SOUL OF RUSSIA

BY THE SAME AUTHOR

La Vie de Michel Bakounine
Gallimard, Paris, 1930

L'Homme Soviétique
Desclée, de Brouwer et Cie, Paris, 1936

Soviet Man—Now
Sheed & Ward, London, 1936

Femmes Soviétiques
Desclée, de Brouwer et Cie, Paris, 1937

Light Before Dusk
Longmans Green & Co., New York, 1942

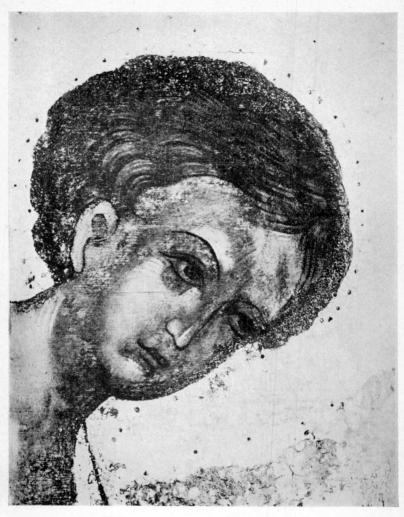

HEAD OF ST. DMITRY BY ANDREW RUBLIV. DETAIL OF
THE ICONOSTAS OF THE TRINITY CATHEDRAL OF THE
TROITSE—SERGIEVA LAVRA. FIRST 30 YEARS OF 15TH
CENTURY

SOUL OF RUSSIA

BY
HELEN ISWOLSKY

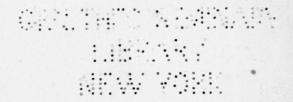

NEW YORK
SHEED & WARD
1943

To
My Mother

Author's Foreword

THIS BOOK might be called an outline of Russia's spiritual history. It has been designed not as an exhaustive study of this subject—for such a study would require several volumes—but as a reference book permitting the reader to see at a glance the salient aspects of Russian religious culture and tradition.

Russia's history is full of struggles. It is not for the first time in a thousand years that she is defending herself against a formidable invader. She has been conquered, occupied, torn to pieces, only to be reintegrated by the spiritual forces which have shaped her destiny. Although the record of events is at times intricate and paradoxical, it may be said that her development has been informed by several invariable principles—the manifestations of a deep religious consciousness on the part of the Russian people.

To the Catholic who wants to know something about his separated brothers, we have tried to show where Catholicism and Orthodoxy can meet and how Russia, in spite of the Schism, is still linked by an invisible bond to the Universal Church.

The reader will not find a discussion of controversial questions in this book, or a history of the attempts at union which have been made and have failed because the time was not ripe or the methods employed impracticable. We have sought to show the forces in Russia herself which have been tending towards *universality* and the directions taken by the apostles of union who have left their mark on Russian thought, such as Yury Krijanitch, the Croat priest, Peter Chaadaiev, Wladimir Soloviev, and such Russian Catholics as have made their contributions to Russian culture. "Union," wrote Wladimir Soloviev, "must be not a mechanical but an organic, chemical process." The Russians whose thought and writings have contributed to this organic process *inside* Russia appear to us as the true pioneers of universality.

Further, we have sought to show the impulses derived from the Russian Orthodox Church at work in that vast country, building Russian unity, kindling the flame of the spirit, rallying the Russian people in times of emergency, and in particular, preserving the old ideal of social justice and human solidarity founded on brotherhood which is the true expression of Russia's soul. It is this ideal which enabled the Russian people to resist the godless onslaught of communism, so that after twenty-five years of persecution they remain a Christian people. And it is this ideal also, we are convinced, which has mobilized all her strength for this present conflict.

Soul of Russia is a work of love more than a work of scholarship. It is meant to offer a series of meditations on Russia's great religious themes as they were expressed by her famous writers and thinkers, by her saints and her heroes. And it is in a spirit of meditation that it has been written. For this, it seems to us, is the only way in which Russia can be spoken of today, when her spiritual destinies are at stake together with the destinies of the entire world. She is taking part in a universal conflict. May she one day take part in a universal peace.

Sources

THE READER will find the sources of the principal quotations in the footnotes of each chapter. For complete data consult the bibliography at the end of the book.

Except for quotations borrowed from available English translations and a number of works of American, English, and French scholars, we have used Russian sources mainly. These can be divided into three categories: the works of Russian scholars and standard editions published in Russia before the Revolution of 1917; the works of Soviet scholars and outstanding Russian authors published after the Revolution in the U.S.S.R. (to this category belong the new edition of Tolstoy's works and the unpublished material discovered in Russian archives and edited by the Moscow Academy in the series "Literaturnoye Nasledstvo"); the works of Russian authors and scholars published abroad by the cultural circles of the emigration. Certain publications, such as the review *Epopeia* appeared simultaneously in the U.S.S.R. and abroad, and these works are dated Moscow-Berlin. Because of this continual reprinting of already published material, to which there are added unpublished essays, letters, and diaries discovered in the Soviet archives, we cannot, in many instances, indicate a "standard" edition. The monumental new edition of Tolstoy's works which is to comprise a hundred volumes and which Soviet research workers began to bring out in 1928, is as yet incomplete, and the old standard editions of Tolstoy's works can by no means be considered complete, since they do not contain much of the material (diaries, rough draughts, and variations) published in the Soviet edition. This is true of

Dostoievsky's works, also. The old standard editions do not contain such important pages of *The Possessed* as "Stavrogin's Confession," published for the first time in the U.S.S.R., and the new full Soviet edition of Dostoievsky is as yet uncompleted. In such cases we list both old and Soviet editions. Moreover, a number of letters of Russian authors and much important biographical material has been published for the first time in the "Literaturnoye Nasledstvo" to which we have referred.

The author had begun the preparation of *Soul of Russia* in Paris and had to leave her notes and bibliography behind when she fled from the French capital in 1940. Some of the books she consulted in the Paris libraries are not available in New York, which accounts for the incompleteness of certain bibliographical data, although the books contained at the Public Library of New York City, the Library of Congress in Washington, D. C., and the library of the University of Chicago furnished her with most of the necessary material.

Contents

List of Illustrations

I

The Birth of a Nation

THE RUSSIAN EMPIRE, which extended over one-sixth of the globe, traced its origin to a handful of Slavonic and Finnish tribes clustering between Lake Ilmen and the Dnieper. These tribes were ruled by Norse princes, the descendants of the Varengian Viking Riurik who founded the Riurikovitch dynasty.[1]

The embryo of the Russian state was formed around the city of Kiev, situated in the midst of the boundless Ukrainian steppes, an area inhabited by constantly moving peoples out for plunder, with no natural barriers to keep them in check. Encircled by these inimical nomads, Russia was forced to repel invasions from the very first centuries of her history.

Beyond the steppes lay Byzantium in all her splendor, for the whole of eastern Europe an almost legendary city, the center of cultural and religious life and the symbol of prosperity. The people of Kiev, the Russ, as they called themselves, were characterized by a spirit of adventure combined with a sound commercial instinct which led them to journey to Constantinople, following the Dnieper, that "great water highway from the Varengians to the Greeks," in order to trade with the Byzantine emperors. The Norse rulers of the Russ, experienced in the art of war, accompanied these commercial

[1] In 862 the tribes inhabiting Russia appealed to Riurik to protect them against the nomads who constantly attacked them during their commercial expeditions. Riurik went to Russia with his two brothers, Sinius and Truver, and his men-at-arms, establishing his rule in Novgorod, one of the most ancient of Russian cities.

expeditions to ward off attacks by the nomads of the steppes. Thus there gradually developed a commercial link between powerful Byzantium and the new-born political and economic entity called Russia. The new state was cemented and consecrated when, on July 15, 988, Prince Wladimir of Kiev baptized his people in the Dnieper.

Scholars often question the validity of the popular legend on which a country's early history is founded; yet we can scarcely disregard legend when it gives expression to the ideals which animate a people. In the story of Russia's evangelization, the authenticity of which has been doubted of late, certain characteristics of the Russian religious temper are discernible.

Prince Wladimir of Kiev, so the story goes, having resolved to renounce his pagan gods, questioned the representatives of various religions as to their respective faiths. When the Moslems told him that they were forbidden the use of wine, the Prince, who was fond of revelling, declared: "Russia delights in drinking; we cannot do without it!" Nor did the Jewish religion satisfy him, for when he asked where their kingdom was, they answered that the wrath of God had dispersed them. Finally, the prince chose the Christian faith. But before making up his mind he sent ambassadors to Rome and Constantinople, ordering them to report what they found there.

The ambassadors returned to relate their experiences. The Roman services had not appealed to them, but when they had arrived in Constantinople and entered St. Sophia they had no longer known "whether they were on earth or in heaven," since on earth "so great a spectacle and so much beauty cannot be seen!" Surely, it was the faith of the Greeks which was the best of all. So, it is related, Prince Wladimir decided to become a member of the Greek Orthodox Church.

This is the version traditionally presented in schoolbooks, but modern scholarship maintains that Prince Wladimir had no need of questioning foreigners in order to be inclined towards Christianity. There had been Christians among the Norse princes and their warriors; two young Varengians, Askold and Dir, had suffered martyrdom at the hands of the pagan Slavs; and Wladimir's own grandmother, Princess Olga, had been baptized. Nor could Wladimir have been obliged to *make a choice* between the Greek and the Roman faiths, because in his day no final schism between Rome and Constantinople had taken place. There was one universal church, and it was this church which Wladimir must have entered with his people.

Nevertheless the rift between East and West was already becoming apparent. Byzantium, in bitter rivalry with Rome, was seeking to extend its influence to all the peoples of eastern Europe, who were gradually being Christianized. As we have seen, Russia, the most important state of that eastern Slavonic world, was already closely linked by trade with Constantinople, and it was to Byzantium and not to far-away Latin Rome that Wladimir would inevitably have turned, even though no schism had yet occurred to create two churches.

It is true that a breach between Rome and Constantinople had been caused in 867 by Patriarch Photius, and this had not been the first of its kind. There had been fifty-five years of schism during the Arian dissensions, eleven years of schism following the deposition of St. John Chrysostom, thirty-five years of Acacian schism, forty-one years of Monothelite schism, and forty-one years of schism due to iconoclasm. But these differences had been caused more by bad feeling than by actual theological dissension between the church in the East and the church in the West. In each instance a compromise was effected, only to have the differences recur, hastening the process of estrangement. But the final break, known as the Great Eastern Schism, was not completed until 1058 under Patriarch Michael Caerularius, ninety-nine years after the patriarchate of Photius.

Wladimir's choice in 988 was not, then, in the matter of dogma, since there was still only one faith, but rather a selection guided by cultural, economic, and political interests. Yet there was a choice in the matter of rite, for already differences in liturgy had developed between the church in the East and the church in the West. The splendors of the Eastern church profoundly impressed the Russian emissaries who entered St. Sophia. That they believed themselves transported into Paradise and listening to a choir of angels' voices is certainly true. This responsiveness to sensible beauty is characteristic of the Russian people's aesthetic approach to religion and the aspiration towards a transfigured world reflecting superhuman harmony, the radiance of the Celestial City in the material world, which has ever informed the Russian spirit. These primitive pagan Slavs and their warrior princes did not possess the erudition necessary to penetrate the theological depths of the Christian faith, but through liturgy they had direct access to a spiritual order of things expressed in terms of beauty. It was their first vision of Christianity, and this vision was to remain forever with the Russian people.

Although the Byzantine church became Russia's mother church, its influence did not prevail in Kiev, as the emperors and prelates of Constantinople had expected. It is typical of the independent spirit of the Russian catechumens that on the eve of his own baptism and that of his people Wladimir led a military expedition against the Byzantine colony of Chersun. It was only after defeating the Greeks and even threatening to destroy their empire that he bound himself to the acceptance of their faith and married the Byzantine emperor's daughter Anne.

For a time Greek metropolitans administered the new Russian church, but eventually a Russian hierarchy supplanted the Greek clergy. We shall further see that the Russian state considered itself neither the political nor the spiritual vassal of Byzantium but rather its *heir,* the guardian of the treasures of the true Christian tradition which had rested in the Greek church since the days of Constantine.

At the early stage we are describing Russian Christianity had not, of course, developed so wide a vision. As yet it closely identified itself with the Greek religious forms, which by that time had become fixed. This static character is admitted by Russian Orthodox thinkers, who have often stressed "Byzantine immobility," pointing out that Russia's mother church had already ceased to be creative when Christianity was brought to Kiev.

The controversy with Rome was absorbing all the life forces of Byzantium, and thus there was being evolved a rigid state religion remote from the dynamic teachings of the Eastern Fathers. The preoccupation of the Eastern clergy was with controversy in regard to theological subtleties far more than with the development of Christian life. There was no place for growth in the immobile framework of this splendid ritualism. Nevertheless the Christianization of Russia, brought about through Byzantium, was an event of the utmost importance. It is a landmark of Russian history.

When Wladimir was baptized and performed his subjects' collective baptism, he may be said to have introduced Russia into the family of great Christian kingdoms. She began to participate in the international life of the period. From then on, Russian princes were in close touch not only with the Byzantine Empire but also with western Europe. They married foreign princesses—Greek, Polish, Hungarian. Through marriage, their daughters became the queens of Western states. Thus, for instance, Princess Anne of Kiev married Henry I of France. Her Slavonic Bible is preserved in Rheims Cathedral. Another Russian princess, Parascevia, who made her home in Rome after a pilgrimage to the Holy Land, led a life of great piety and was canonized by Pope Gregory X.

We must think of Christian Russia of that time, that is, in the tenth and eleventh centuries and even into the twelfth, as open to influences from both Rome and Byzantium. St. Boniface and St. Bruno as well as the Greek missionaries evangelized the people of Kiev. Both Rome and Constantinople sent their ambassadors to the court of the Russian princes. The Pope received Prince Jaropolk, one of Wladimir's successors. The Holy See dispatched its delegates to Kiev with the relics of St. Clement, and the shrine of St. Nicholas at Bari in Italy was venerated by the Russians. There was continuous intercourse, both spiritual and political, between the East and the West.

A superficial knowledge of early Russian history has misrepresented the Kiev state as an Asiatic princedom closed to European influences. Today a more profound historical research gives evidence that medieval Russia had already reached a high level of Christian culture. It was a country very much like the other Christian countries of its time. This cultural growth was to be checked only by the Mongol invasion in the thirteenth century. It was the Mongol conqueror who brought the Asiatic strain to Russia, and even he did not succeed in uprooting the seeds of Christian civilization sown in the previous centuries.

Before the Mongol invasion Russia's commerce and industry were prosperous; her customs corresponded with a profoundly ethical code; her princes were enlightened, just, and charitable. One of them, Jaroslav the Wise, who reigned in the eleventh century, compiled a body of laws inspired with high Christian ideals, known as the *Russian Truth*. Another famous ruler, Wladimir Monomakhos, is known in history as the "brother-loving prince and friend of the poor."

The early Russian state was not an autocracy like the Muscovite Empire founded a few centuries later. Kiev, Novgorod, and the other thriving cities of those days were governed by the *Vetche,* an elected body which not only advised the prince but regulated his activity.

As we have seen, the fixed forms of Byzantine ritualism lent the Russian church an apparent immobility; but the spirit of Russian Christianity was far from static; it was a dynamic factor in the growth of Russian civilization.

One of the reasons for this dynamism is the fact that the Russian church used the native vernacular in its services. The use of the Slavonic tongue, introduced to the liturgy by Saints Cyrill and Methodius, had finally received Papal sanction, despite the vigorous opposition of the German bishops and all the champions of Latinism. Thus the Russians took on the characteristics of the other Christianized Slavonic peoples. The common people made the newly acquired faith a part of themselves. Byzantine scholarship and theology were not accessible to their simple minds, but the Gospel truths were conveyed to them through the prayers and sacred books translated into their own tongue, and Christianity permeated the Russian consciousness. Wladimir's ambassadors had beheld the magnificence of the Eastern rite as a reflection of unearthly beauty, but to the people who were to constitute the Russian nation there was made a further revelation: They had a spontaneous vision of the Christian ideal. And this vision was so true, so vivid, that it impressed the Russian soul for all the centuries to come.

Historians of the Russian church have studied attentively the origins and growth of Russian Christianity during the early Kiev period. They have stressed its influence on Russian culture and the contribution which it made to the gradual formation of Russian medieval theocracy, which was to attain full development in the Muscovite Empire. But it is only during recent years that scholars have looked at the inner aspect of early Russian Christianity in the effort to apprehend the hidden spirit which kindled the soul of the newly baptized people. And they have made the remarkable discovery that even in these primitive times there existed a religious impulse which had not originated in Byzantine fixed forms but was innately Russian. This impulse, which has continued to make itself felt throughout the succeeding centuries, is the wellspring of the religious and social aspirations that revealed themselves in the nineteenth and twentieth centuries.

The first Russian saints were Wladimir and Olga, the rulers of Kiev. The first Russians to be canonized after Wladimir were his sons Boris and Gleb. In the story of the two brothers a religious motif which is peculiarly Russian can be discerned. Attacked by their elder brother, who wanted to rule supreme in Kiev, Boris and Gleb ordered their men-at-arms to offer no resistance, preferring death to civil strife. Thus the ideal of nonresistance to evil was articulated ten centuries before Tolstoy.

Although they were worshipped by their people and possessed, it seems, all the attributes of sanctity, the canonization of Boris and Gleb encountered many obstacles. Their case was difficult to classify. They had been exemplary Christians and had died heroic deaths. Yet, although Boris had said, "If I am slain by my brother, I shall be martyr to my God," the two brothers could not be considered martyrs for the Christian faith in the accepted sense. They had not preached the Gospels or performed miracles; their only extraordinary action had consisted in the meekness and self-abandonment with which they had met brute force. The Greek hierarchy was confused and reluctant to act, but finally the Russian clergy prevailed, and Boris and Gleb were canonized as *strastoterptzy* (i.e., passion-bearers), a term coined by the Russians to define the quality of the young men's sanctity. There is something in this early tale which seems to foreshadow the mystical humanism of Dostoievsky.

Another example of primitive Russian mysticism is found in St. Theodosius, abbot of the Petchersky *Laura,* the famous abbey of Kiev. As a child Theodosius was in the care of his mother, the widow of a wealthy landowner, but at an early age he left his high position to labor with the serfs in the fields, assuming their burdens and sharing their underprivileged life. He was, one might say, the first Russian who "went to the people," and as such is the precursor of the nineteenth century intelligentsia who left the society of which they were a part to share the life of the peasant.

When St. Theodosius retired to the Petchersky Monastery, he followed the tradition of the Fathers of the Desert, the great hermits of Egypt. The abbey was famous for its mortifications. The monks lived in caves and underground cells; they were practically walled-in, wearing heavy chains and bound to solitude, silence, and severe fasting. Theodosius mitigated the austerities of the rule, applying the teaching of St. Savva, a Palestinian father of the sixth century who had opposed extreme mortification. The Palestine school taught the "middle way"; it prescribed "spiritual soberness," that is, a life of prayer and manual labor, of harmony and balance excluding excesses of religious fervor. The monk was to be "an earthly angel, an angelic man," the image of celestial peace, not of fanatical self-torture.

Theodosius led his brethren out of their dark underground caves into the light. He instituted community life and agricultural labor. He would himself rise at night to grind the flour and bake the bread of the brethren. But the essential rule observed by this saint was poverty. He exemplified the so-called *kenotic* conception of Christianity, which present-day Russian theologians describe as the characteristic trait of the Russian religious spirit.[2] The Greek word *kenosis,* meaning evacuation or self-emptying, is borrowed from St. Paul's epistle to the Philippians II, 5–7:

For let this mind be in you, which was also in Christ Jesus: Who being in the form of God, thought it not robbery to be equal with God: But *emptied* himself, taking the form of a

[2] The Russian Orthodox concept of *kenosis* must not be confused with the heretical theory of Protestant divines, according to which God the Son, in becoming man, discarded his divinity. To the Russian church *kenosis* refers simply to the stripping and emptying of self implied in spiritual poverty. See Fedotov, G. P., *The Religious Sources of Russian Populism.*

servant, being made in the likeness of men and in habit found as a man.

Even at that early stage of its development, Russian mysticism worshipped the Christ who, divesting himself of His divine Glory, put on the "poor garb" of humanity. And this was precisely the ideal of Theodosius. Even in his youth, when living in the house of his wealthy mother, he had worn "poor and patched clothing," saying that rich garments were "a heavy burden upon him." Rebuked by his mother for working in the fields with the serfs, he had declared that he wished to be "as one of the poor," for "Our Lord Jesus Christ Himself became poor and humble, giving us the example that we may also humiliate ourselves for His sake."

Theodosius, as we have seen, sought not so much bodily mortification as *self-identification with the despised and the oppressed*. He is one of the founders of the Russian humanist tradition which was to fertilize the Russian imagination throughout the centuries until it bore fruit in the literary and religious masterpieces of Russian thought.

II

Builders of Russia

FROM THE TENTH CENTURY to the time of the Mongol invasion Kiev was the cultural center of Russia. It was Kiev's monastic clergy which fostered this culture—spiritual, ethical, literary, and artistic. The Petchersky Monastery, founded in the eleventh century, was the cradle of Russian monasticism, the source of the religious dynamism of the period. The lives of its most famous monks, collected in a volume entitled the *Paterikon*, were eagerly read by the Russian people.

In reviewing the development of the monastic life of that time we should not seek to compare it with Western or Greek patterns. The fact that the Slavonic tongue was used in the liturgy and in preaching, while contributing to the rapid spread of religion among the common people, rendered the study of Greek and Latin unnecessary; thus Russia was cut off from the sources of theological erudition. Her monks and priests were not classical scholars; their piety was founded on the Holy Scriptures, the Psalter, and such moral teachings of St. John Chrysostom and St. John Damascene as had been translated. Plato and Aristotle, whose philosophies Latin and Greek Christianity had already absorbed, were not to influence Russian religious thought until many centuries later, when seminaries of the Western type were founded in the chief Russian cities.

This does not mean that the monasticism practiced in Kiev was of an inferior kind. It was cruder perhaps, and less evolved than the monasticism of the West; it was not a rule of life formed according to the strict intellectual discipline derived from metaphysical studies. But it trod the mystical path of the great Fathers of the Desert, and thus it was able to produce remarkable personalities like St. Theodosius.

If the monks of the Petchersky Monastery were not students of Greek philosophy, there were nevertheless many learned men among them. The first Russian chronicler was St. Nestor of the Petchersky *Laura* and his work was continued throughout the centuries by other religious of the various monasteries. These ancient Russian chronicles are precious historical documents; they are furthermore the expression of the political, religious, and ethical concepts which cemented the Russian state. In describing historical events and characterizing the Kiev rulers, the Petchersky monks continually stressed the role of divine providence in human affairs and the necessity of obedience to the laws of God. The ideal prince should possess not only military skill and political far-sightedness but also the highest moral virtues: justice, charity, piety, fortitude, and devotion to his people. The chronicles reflect the conviction that spiritual forces should shape the national destiny; thus they are concerned with the political as well as with the spiritual condition of the Russian state.

However, the beneficent influence of the church was not strong enough to counterbalance the great violence of the times; civil strife continually flared up between the rival branches of the Riurikovitch dynasty. Russia had not yet attained unity. She was divided into princedoms, each governed by a ruler belonging to the house of Riurik. The senior prince occupied the seat of Kiev, but his throne was continually disputed by his brothers and cousins. This family struggle shook the very foundations of the Russian state. The end of the twelfth century marked the decline of Kiev and the rise of the city of Wladimir, which became Russia's capital. But scarcely fifty years had elapsed after the eclipse of Kiev when

Russia entered the sombre period of the Mongol invasion, the greatest calamity of her history.

In 1223 the armies of Prince Mstislav Galitzky were defeated on the river Kalka by Chingis-Khan's lieutenants Tchepe and Subudai. In 1236 Chingis-Khan's successor, Baty, marched on Europe, sweeping through Russia. Moscow, which at that time was but a small town of no political importance, was captured by the invader. Then the Mongols besieged Wladimir, the new capital. After the fall of this city the cathedral was burned and the metropolitan perished in the flames. Yury, the ruling prince of Wladimir, was killed in the battle on the river Syte in 1238, and his death led to the final defeat of the Russians. In 1240 Baty devastated Kiev and the adjoining cities, overran Poland, and invaded Hungary and Silesia. His drive was checked in Moravia, whence he turned back and established his headquarters at Sarai, in the southern steppes of Russia, on the banks of the Akhtir River, a tributary of the Volga.

The Mongol invasion wrought havoc in Russia, checking her normal development for two centuries. The ruling classes, the secular clergy, and the monks fled from the cities. Princes were turned into vassals of the Mongol masters, obliged to pay homage to the conquerors and to worship the heathen gods. If they refused, they were slain outright or poisoned. The people were enslaved and made to pay heavy tribute. Long after the actual invasion was over and Baty settled down at Sarai, they trembled in vivid recollection of the murder and plunder which had marked the wake of the invader.

Religious life, which had already yielded remarkable fruit, was submerged by the wave of brutality and bloody warfare. Yet the Mongol onslaught, terrible as it was, did not have the destruction of Christianity as one of its aims. Although the Mongols were exacting masters, exercising absolute military and political authority, they were as a rule tolerant towards religion, and except for the fact that the defeated princes who were led into Sarai were made to kneel before the Khans and their idols, no further attempt was made to enforce pagan gods on the conquered people. The invaders did not seek to stifle the spirit of the vassal nation as long as the required tribute was forthcoming. This truly providential circumstance permitted the church to rise from the cinders and regain its strength, although on certain occasions, it suffered from the Mongol yoke and had to struggle against the invader.

Fourteen years after Prince Yury's defeat, his nephew Alexander was placed on the throne in the city of Wladimir. Prince Alexander, whom the Russian church canonized, personified the high virtues which the chronicles imputed to the ideal Christian prince. He brilliantly reaffirmed Russian national and spiritual values. A courageous warrior and an expert general, he combined shrewdness with a quality of rapid decision. Alexander defeated the Swedes, who at that time were attempting to invade Russia. He won a no less decisive victory over the Knights of the Teutonic Order, on the icebound Lake of Tchud.

As the chronicles describe the methods of these Western warriors with their formidable steel-clad, heavily armed units they somehow remind one of the technique exhibited by modern blitz-krieg and panzer divisions. Alexander had no such effective equipment, but his troops were well trained and eager to fight in defense of their land, inspired by the motto inscribed on their prince's banner: "God is not in strength, but in truth." Even today in communist Russia the memory of Alexander's victory is alive. He is venerated as a national hero. In December, 1942, Metropolitan Nicholas of Kiev quoted the words of this thirteenth-century saint, whose motto has become the symbol of Russian national defense throughout the centuries, in his Christmas message to the Soviet people.

The Swedes and Teutonic Knights withdrew from Russian territory. Their defeat proved that the Russians, though suffering under the Mongol yoke, were still conscious of their national unity and intent upon guarding their Western frontiers. Victory not only stimulated Russia patriotism but reawakened religious feeling, for the Teutonic Knights were Latins, and their invasion was regarded as an attempt to implant Catholicism in Russia. Soon after the Tchud battle, Pope Innocent IV dispatched delegates to Alexander in an attempt to persuade the Russian prince to unite himself with Rome. The prince replied that although he was well informed of all that had happened from the creation of the world to the seventh council, he rejected the "teaching of the Latins."

Thus ended the endeavor which would have brought Roman Catholicism to Russia. The fact that this armed force had represented Catholicism naturally provoked the distrust and hostility of the Wladimir ruler and his people. From that day on, the Latins were looked upon as invaders, seeking territorial as well as spiritual gains. But as D. Tolstoy, the historian of Catholicism in Russia, points out, Alexander's reply to the Pope, even though referring to the unacceptable "Latin teachings," did not stress the dogmatic differences existing between the Roman Catholic and the Orthodox churches. He seems to have been aware only of the differences in rite and language— most of all of the fact that Roman Catholicism was the faith of his enemies. This antagonism towards the representatives of Latinism was to embitter all future relations between the Russian Orthodox Church and Rome.

Alexander was now convinced that he was strong enough to resist invasion from the West. But there was still Baty to cope with in the East. The Russian prince's father, who had resisted the Mongol tyrant, had died of poisoning. Other members of the Riurikovitch dynasty had either fled to Hungary and Poland or bowed to the conqueror, becoming, so to speak, collaborationists. Alexander neither imitated his father's stiff-necked resistance nor adopted a servile attitude. He went to the Khan's court at Sarai bringing Baty many offerings, but as a warrior fresh from victory, not as a vanquished prince. Baty had heard of the defeat of the Swedes and the Teutonic Knights. Alexander's personality impressed him. "All I have been told about the prince is true," the Khan declared; "this man has no rival."

Alexander observed the etiquette demanded of Baty's vassals. He was docile and conciliatory. Yet he obtained from the Khan a concession essential to Russia's ultimate liberation: henceforth, taxes would be collected not by Baty's Mongol officials but by the Russian princes themselves. Prince Alexander Nevsky (thus called because of his victory over the Swedes on the Neva River) died on his way home from Sarai. He was mourned by his people, and the Metropolitan of Wladimir exclaimed: "The Sun of the Russian land hath set!" Canonized in the fifteenth century, Alexander has become one of Russia's most venerated saints. As we have seen, the Soviet Government considers him the national hero who symbolizes the country's spirit of patriotism and unity. A recent Soviet film features the battle on Lake Tchud, with a great display of Russian warriors worsting the steel-clad Teutonic Knights. Many historical and biographical essays have been devoted to this medieval prince by Soviet scholars. Naturally, these writers do not dwell on Alexander's virtues as a saint: "He combined sober shrewdness with the brilliance of knightly valor. As a defender of Russia's territory, he was not a soft-hearted Christian, devoted to his neighbor's welfare. He was an austere lord, absorbed in the development of his economy, of his land. His deep devotion to its needs made this prince a leader of his people." [1]

And yet, the enthusiasm which the name of Alexander Nevsky still awakens in Russia is scarcely inspired by this austerity and shrewdness. The common people have preserved another picture of their favorite saint. In the *Acaphist,* an ancient votive prayer of the Russian church, Alexander is

[1] Khmelnitzky, *Alexander Nevsky i ego Vermia.*

called "the feeder of the hungry, the defender of the weak." Essentially a Christian prince, he was conscious of an ethical mission inspired by a lofty ideal, the ideal of the Russian people, for whom God is not in strength but in truth.

Although Alexander Nevsky rekindled Russia's national and religious spirit after the Mongol invasion, it was not until the second part of the fourteenth century that the Mongols suffered military defeat at the hands of the Russians. At that time the city of Wladimir was no longer the seat of the supreme ruler. The capital had been transferred to Moscow, which had escaped destruction. Alexander's son Daniel and later his grandson Yury were the first reigning princes of Moscow. These rulers began to acquire new territories through war, legacy, or marriage. The metropolitan's seat was also transferred to Moscow at that time.

One of the first Moscow prelates, Peter, who did much to protect the Russian church during the period of subjection to the Mongol, visited the Khans in Sarai and established relations with them with the aim of obtaining greater religious freedom for Russia. He was canonized as "the sufferer for the Russian land." Metropolitan Peter predicted that if a church were built in Moscow in honor of the Holy Virgin, and if he were buried in its vaults, the city would become large and prosperous and its rulers would grow to be more powerful than all other princes. The church was built and this prophecy realized.

Peter died under the rule of Prince John Kalita, who has been called the "collector of Russian land." The word Kalita (meaning "a purse" in Greek) symbolized the statesmanship and prudence of this thrifty prince, who was continually accumulating riches and acquiring new territories. Though the chronicles describe him as using his purse to distribute alms to the needy, he was certainly as careful with his spending as he was shrewd and businesslike in extending his boundaries. At the end of his reign, he called himself Prince of all Russia, and when his son Simeon mounted the throne, Moscow was indeed the capital of a powerful and wealthy state.

It was at about that time, in the early fourteenth century, that three remarkable men were born: One was Kalita's grandson, Dmitry, who became prince of Moscow; the other two were Alexis, who was to become Metropolitan of Moscow, and Sergius, founder of the famous Troitzky Monastery of Radonezh and one of Russia's greatest spiritual builders.

While studying this period, we shall have little to say about relations with the Catholic world. Russia had been practically cut off from western Europe by the Mongol invasion. Moreover, the Great Eastern Schism was now complete, and Byzantium's final rift with Rome had, naturally, a decisive effect on the Russian church. Although the Russian high clergy did not officially condemn Rome, a growing hostility towards the Western church developed. We have seen how Alexander Nevsky rejected Pope Innocent's offer. Russian princes who formed alliances with the Latins, that is, with the Poles or the Lithuanians, were subsequently considered renegades. For a time Roman missionaries continued to come to Russia, but they were not welcomed as in the Kiev period, and eventually they were forbidden to enter Moscow. Latin monks occasionally reached not only the Muscovite state but even the Mongol's domain, where they met Russian princes paying homage to the Khans. But it can be said of that period that no intercourse in spiritual matters existed between East and West; such accidental encounters as took place between Roman and Orthodox Christians exercised no influence on Russian religious life.

The latter continued to develop purely according to Orthodox tendencies. The emancipation of the Russian people from the Mongol yoke was a gradual, extremely slow process, but it went on under John Kalita and his successors and gained in strength under Prince Dmitry. While this young ruler was growing to manhood in Moscow and learning the arts of war and statesmanship, Sergius, the devout son of a Rostov nobleman, went into the wilderness to lead a hermit's life. He was at that time barely twenty, and he was to spend many years in solitude before linking his name to Russia's historical destiny.

Sergius, as was then the custom for those who chose the eremitical life, built himself a frame hut and a chapel in the thick woods forty miles from Moscow, where he led a solitary existence of prayer and mortification. Gradually, he was joined by other hermits, and his northern *thebaide* ("desert") was founded. Unlike the monks who were satisfied with the knowledge of the Slavonic liturgy and books of piety, Sergius spoke Greek and was a scholar. A man of rich interior life and comprehensive vision, he was able to exercise extraordinary discernment in the building up of his community.

The Troitzky Monastery of Radonezh, erected on the site of the early *thebaide,* was to become one of the most influential of Russian religious centers. Nevertheless the character of the Abbot Sergius showed no diminution of the humility which was his salient grace. He is one of the most remarkable representatives of kenotic Christianity. Of all the monks of his community he was the poorest in spirit, most tireless and mortified. His clothes were patched, his appearance gave evidence of severe privation. When he prescribed manual labor to his monks as their only means of subsistence, he worked with them in order to gain his daily bread. It is related that one day, being without food, he built a cell for one of the monks and received in payment a basket of rotten apples. On another occasion he was grossly insulted by a peasant calling at the monastery, who mistook the abbot for a beggar. Before every visitor, Sergius prostrated himself, beholding in each man the image of God. He treated his brethren with so much meekness that the hagiograph describes him as "an abbot without power." He acted as cook, baker, miller, woodcutter, and carpenter of the community. He addressed the novices in gentle and affectionate tones even when they deserved rebuke. This does not mean, however, that he lacked the gifts of a spiritual director. He moulded his monks' souls unerringly and produced a generation of religious who were to play a prominent role in Russia's spiritual revival.

What Sergius taught his monks first of all was holy poverty. A pilgrim who had heard wondrous tales about the Troitzky Monastery and who visited their shrine, thus described what he found there: "Everything bears the stamp of indigence, all are as beggars and orphans." It was indeed a *thebaide* in the true sense of the word. The great trees of the primitive forest rustled at the abbey's gate and shed their leaves on the rough-hewn roof. In winter the buildings were snow-bound, completely cut off from the outside world. Wild beasts roamed in the woods, but Sergius tamed even the bears and the wolves. Though the brethren often went without bread, there was always enough to feed the poor. The monks "ate the bark of the trees and mowed the grass of the swamps," the chronicler relates. "Even the church was poor and bare. Wherever you looked, everything was amiss." [2]

The saintly abbot's fame soon spread throughout Russia. Pilgrims flocked to the monastery and powerful princes and noblemen came to seek Sergius' advice. Thanks to his wisdom and prudence, affairs of state were settled and civil strife avoided. His gentle but firm persuasion led Oleg of Riazan, one of the most turbulent and stubborn princes of the time, to sign "eternal peace" with Moscow. This act further cemented the supremacy of the Moscow princes and put an end to civil war. But Sergius' greatest practical achievement was to kindle Russia's desire for the freedom from her Mongol oppressors, which he felt to be essential to his people's spiritual fulfilment. He showed great prudence in the beginning. When Prince Dmitry first consulted him about the attitude to be adopted

[2] See Fedotov, *Sviatye Drevnei Russi*; Zernov, *St. Sergius, Builder of Russia*; Klyuchevsky, *A History of Russia*, Vol. II.

towards the Khans, Sergius replied: "Submit to the ruler." But when Moscow was strong enough for effective resistance, it was Sergius who inspired the prince with the final determination to set his people free.

Dmitry had been reared in an atmosphere calculated to strengthen his hostility towards the Mongols. Metropolitan Alexis, his tutor and close adviser, was himself imbued with the spirit of emancipation: "Remove the yoke from the Russian land, Dmitry," he would tell the prince, "and if thou succeedest in breaking yet another strap of this yoke, thou shalt be blessed. . . ."

Under the tutelage of the metropolitan, who was experienced in statesmanship and who never ceased to guide and encourage the young prince, Dmitry prepared himself for the great task of becoming Moscow's liberator. In certain ways he resembled his grandfather, Kalita. He was careful in spending and interested in the expansion and consolidation of his territories. He was expert in military science and a trained soldier. Simply clad, he did not care for the splendors of the Byzantine attire which Russia's ruling princes had recently adopted.

Ties of friendship linked the royal tutor with the saint in the wilderness. Dmitry also sought out the Abbot of Radonezh, and after the death of Alexis, he offered Sergius the metropolitan's seat. Although the hermit rejected this honor, he went to Moscow to confer with the prince and not only blessed Dmitry's undertakings but urged him to take immediate action: "In his ragged clothes," writes one of his biographers, "covered with the dust of the roads, enveloped in the glory of wisdom and saintliness, he was more powerful than all the princes, and than the metropolitan himself." [3] Curiously enough, these lines were written by Borodin, a Soviet author. For like Alexander Nevsky, Sergius of Radonezh and Dmitry Donskoy are considered national heroes in Soviet Russia and unquestionably the best historical work devoted to them is

[3] Borodin, *Dmitry Donskoy*.

from the pen of this Communist writer. There is a continuity in Russia's historical evolution, or rather in her spiritual dynamism, which even the godless authors cannot ignore.

At the time when Dmitry sought Sergius' blessing, hidden forces had already prepared Russia for independence, and the encouragement of the Abbot of Radonezh quickened his people's aspirations. For many years they had trembled at the very name of the Khans, but Sergius had revived not only religious faith but national fortitude.

In 1378 Prince Dmitry led his armies to the Riazan principality, which was suffering a new Mongol onslaught. He promised help and protection to the Riazan prince, who, once his bitterest enemy, was now, as a result of Sergius' mediation, his friend and ally. Mamai, the commander of the Mongol army, was defeated, but allying himself with the Lithuanians he threw fresh forces against Dmitry. The Moscow prince assembled a large host reinforced by all the northeastern principalities. Once more he visited Sergius. Then he returned to his army accompanied by two monks from the Troitzky Monastery. Mamai was again defeated on the field of Kulikovo, by the Don River. Although Mongol domination was to last until the fifteenth century, the battle of Kulikovo actually marked the beginning of its decline.

III

Seekers of Silence

ST. SERGIUS of Radonezh has been called **Russia's greatest**
saint. Today he is venerated by both the Russian Orthodox
Church and Russian Catholics of the Eastern rite. Many of the
characteristics of this remarkable monk and the communities
which he founded remind us of St. Benedict. For instance, the
adoration of the Trinity, which constituted one of the chief
devotional exercises in Benedictine monasteries, was also practiced at the Troitzky Monastery, the name of which means
Trinity in the Russian language.

We have seen that the Troitzky abbot started a revival of
national and religious feeling which emancipated Russia from
the Mongol yoke. Quite unintentionally, he became the pioneer
in another important movement, the colonization of the northern wilderness.

The saint of Radonezh who "ate the bark of trees and
mowed the grass of the swamps" with his early brethren left at
his death a powerful community at Radonezh and twenty-
seven other monasteries which he had founded. Many of his
disciples followed his example by becoming solitary contemplatives. They were called the "Seekers of Silence." Like
Sergius, they built their cells in the desert and practiced great
austerities; and they, too, were presently joined by other hermits in whose company they formed the nuclei of new communities. The hermits felled trees and tilled the soil; manual
labor, especially agriculture, was their chief source of livelihood
and also their means to spiritual perfection. Pilgrims and a few

of the peasants of the vicinity joined them in their labors, and thus the wilderness of Russia was gradually opened to agriculture and to religious teaching, the products of Russian civilization.

Inevitably there would come a time when the Seekers of Silence would find community life too worldly. The crowds of pilgrims and wealthy visitors hindered contemplation. Again the monks would set forth in quest of the solitude essential to their way of life. And again their hermitages would attract pious souls and other communities would crop up in the desert, bringing civilization to a new area. During the two centuries following Sergius' death, one hundred forty communities were founded in this manner, the most important being the Abbey of Solovetzk. This famous monastery, located on an island of the White Sea, was erected on the site of the primitive cell built by one of St. Sergius' disciples, Savvaty. The abbey became a great spiritual center and a treasury of art. Centuries later, under the Bolshevists, it was turned into a concentration camp, one of the most dreaded prisons of the Guepeou, where a great number of Orthodox bishops and priests as well as members of the Catholic clergy were interned during the years of anti-religious persecution. Other important spiritual and cultural centers were the Trifono-Petchneg and Valaam monasteries on the Finnish coast, which were the outgrowth of the early evangelization of primitive heathen tribes by St. Sergius' followers.

The Seekers of Silence were men of remarkable religious energies, bound to holy poverty and leading the arduous lives of apostles and pioneers. They endured great self-imposed privations, and although they were the founders of large communities which were to become economically powerful, they themselves never ceased to resent the worldliness which inevitably sprang up around their sanctuaries. As St. Sergius expressed it, this worldliness "disfigured the desert." So the Seekers of Silence penetrated deeper and deeper into the wilderness.

ST. SERGIUS AND HIS MONKS WORKING AND TEACHING

ST. WLADIMIR, SOVEREIGN OF RUSSIA, A. D. 981, WHO ESTABLISHED CHRISTIANITY IN RUSSIA

Some of them became vagrants, like Paul, a disciple of Sergius who wandered for fifty years and Cyril Novoozersky, who lived for twenty years among the wild beasts of the forest.

St. Sergius and his followers, then, were the unwitting leaders of that powerful movement which was carrying Russian civilization northward towards the "frozen seas." In spite of themselves, they were contributing to Russia's economic and political expansion. It is a strange coincidence that these mystics and ascetics who had left the world should have become the instruments by which Moscow extended her influence and founded her northern empire. Even the Bolshevist godless have been forced to admit that the early Russian church represented an important factor in social and cultural progress.

As we have seen, early monastic life drew its impulse from genuine religious experience and was disciplined by asceticism, but the monasticism of later periods was to become infected by worldly motives. The monasteries founded in the wilderness developed into large, wealthy agricultural estates extending over many acres and cultivated by thousands of serfs who labored in the place of the monks and their pious followers. Rich benefactors endowed these foundations with more land and more money in order that when the donors died continual prayers might be said for their souls. Thus from a humble communal life, the monks turned themselves to large-scale agriculture for the production of wealth. Russian historians refer to them as the "black-cassock aristocracy." Inevitably, the spiritual flame began to dwindle, discipline wavered, and asceticism was relaxed. The meaning of kenotic Christianity seemed to be lost. The northern *thebaides* ceased to provide a stimulus to fervor, for they produced no saints to mould the souls of the monks so that they might become angelic men.

The Russian monasteries, conducted in accordance with the rule of St. Basil (St. Benedict's spiritual father and teacher), followed Eastern patterns. Unlike the West, Russia did not produce a variety of religious orders. There was only one type of community, and its monastic life was prescribed by Greek tradition.[1] There was no minutely drafted code, no rule vesting authority in the person of a superior. As in St. Sergius' case, the abbot was often "without power." If he were a spiritual man he sought mortification and humility; if he were of a practical turn of mind, he became the thrifty manager of a wealthy and productive estate; but in neither case did he exercise explicit authority over the brethren. Of course, this does not mean that monastic life was formless. A saint like Sergius conducted his community towards perfection by spiritual means. The power which radiated from his remarkable soul produced a number of extraordinary personalities who spread his influence throughout Russia. Moreover, another type of spiritual discipline, the so-called *Startchestwo*, was also exercising its influence on the religious life of that day. The *Startzy* were spiritual directors chosen among monks or hermits of particularly austere and saintly life who, without exercising the prerogatives of abbots, were called to form the souls of religious and laymen. Startchestwo is an exclusively Orthodox religious pattern which has evolved original methods of mystical and ascetical life.[2] The Startzy demanded absolute obedience; they prescribed austerities which were in some instances infinitely more severe than those of Western monasticism. But this way of life could be followed only by a spiritual élite. Startzys and saints were rare, and as the monasteries spread their network

[1] In spite of the gradual independence gained by the Russian church and the accompanying estrangement between Greeks and Russians, Greek ascetic traditions brought from the famous monastery of Mount Athos still prevailed in Russian communities, mitigated, as we have seen, by the Russian concept of the middle way.

[2] *Startzy* means "elders" in Russian, and the word describes their main attributes: wisdom, experience, the high virtues required for teaching the spiritual way of life, and the practice of asceticism. Although the Startzy were usually religious, some of them were laymen, like the famous Siberian hermit of the nineteenth century Fedor Kozmitch, believed to have been none other than Tsar Alexander I who had retired to an out-of-the-way Siberian town to lead a pious life, while his death was rumored in the capital. See Chapter X.

throughout Russia, the worldly spirit dominated the ascetic one.

The black-cassock aristocracy continued to acquire great economic and political influence, until the princes, and later the tsars, began to look upon them as powerful and even dangerous competitors. The days of the great Seekers of Silence were past.

In justice, however, it must be said that these rapidly growing, powerful communities were not wholly absorbed in temporal concerns. They were cultural centers which fostered the growth of the liturgy, religious art, music, and architecture. There were famous ikon painters among the monks, and some of their works, such as Rublev's ikon of the Trinity, are masterpieces of the highest artistic merit and of a genuine mystical inspiration. Beautifully decorated churches and monasteries containing the most precious art treasures mark the path of Russian religious expansion.

Even when the days of the great saints were past, monastic communities continued to yield spiritual direction. They preserved the ancient ideal of the Christian prince; they defended just causes and prescribed charity to the ruler who had hardened his heart against his subjects; and they were alert to their duty of feeding the poor, their motto being: "The riches of the church are the riches of the beggars." Thus the frequent accusation that Russian monastic communities neglected the active forms of charity is without foundation in fact. It is true that no orders were formed explicitly for charitable purposes, but every monastery was a hostel, a haven for the poor and disabled. The people sought refuge in the early desert hermitages and in the vast abbeys which rose to replace them. St. Joseph of Volokolamsk, who is considered the most typical steward of the black-cassock aristocracy's economic prosperity, did not neglect the poor. He fed from six hundred to seven hundred beggars daily; in times of famine, their numbers increased to about seven thousand. It was one of the most sacred duties of the monasteries to feed the victims of famine. During the severe droughts which frequently devastated the crops and which, under all regimes, have been the scourge of Russia, these religious bodies literally saved the population from starvation.

Here again, we find in medieval Russian Christians the precursors of the later Russian humanists. As one considers in the light of the past the late nineteenth century writings of Tolstoy on the subject of famine, it becomes apparent that his thought stems from early Russian religious teaching and practice. Tolstoy actively participated in the relief work to which all social-minded members of the intelligentsia lent their zeal and energies. For this intelligentsia, as for Tolstoy himself, the sufferings of the starving peasantry were a source of constant mortification.

The economic growth of the monasteries coincided with the development and growth of the church. As the Mongol yoke weakened, the ecclesiastical hierarchy of Moscow underwent a process of stabilization, becoming a strong national church, and as such, the pillar of the state. This process was hastened by two important events which rendered the Russian church independent of Byzantium. The first was the Florentine Union, which effected a reconciliation between Constantinople and Rome. The Metropolitan of Moscow, Isidore, himself a Greek, attended the Council of Florence and gave his support to the Union. He returned to his metropolitan's seat "bringing back the Latin cross" and a prayer for the Pope. The clergy of Moscow protested, Isidore was deposed and placed under arrest, and the ruling prince of Moscow wrote to the Byzantine emperor, Constantine Paleologus, demanding the right to have metropolitans consecrated in Russia. His letter was never answered, for on May 29, 1453 the Greek emperor was killed by the Turks on the ramparts of Constantinople. The fall of Byzantium was looked upon in Russia as just punishment for the "sin of union," since this spiritual surrender to the Latins had been followed by the Moslem conquest of Constantinople. Moscow now considered herself the only defender of the true faith. This conviction was expressed by the monk Philotheus, abbot of a Pskov monastery, who wrote to the prince of Moscow:

"The Church of ancient Rome fell because of Apollinarian heresy. As to the second Rome [meaning Constantinople], it has been hewn down by the axes of the Ishmaelites. But this third Rome, the Holy Apostolic Church, under thy mighty rule shines throughout the entire world more brightly than the sun. . . . Two Romes have fallen, but the third stands and no fourth can ever be."

Recognition of this concept is fundamental to the understanding of Russian religious thought. The Russian church considered not only the Latins but even the Greeks unworthy of sustaining the pure flame of Christianity. In order to lend weight to this contention, the memory of St. Andrew the Apostle who, it was said, had come to evangelize Russia long before the baptism of Wladimir by the Greeks, was revived. When, in the sixteenth century, the Jesuit Possevin came to Moscow as Papal Legate and tried to persuade Tsar John the Terrible to imitate the example of the Greeks and seek union with Rome, the Tsar answered:

"Why do you point out the Greeks to us? Greeks are no Gospel to us; we believe not in the Greeks but in Christ. We received the Christian faith at the birth of the Christian Church, when Andrew brother of Peter came to these parts. . . . Thus we in Moscow embraced the true faith at the same times as you did in Italy and have kept it inviolate from then to the present day."

This consciousness of Russia as the Bearer of the Faith developed under the Mongol yoke, when Moscow was practically cut off from the Byzantine Empire and was drawing her religious inspiration from her own sources. And we have also seen that at the very beginning of her Christianization Russia developed her own religious idiom, her own concepts of sanctity and the perfect life, which were very different from the products of the Greek mentality. As to the Latin West, Moscow was drifting further and further from it. The sack of Constantinople by the crusaders in the twelfth century had left burning traces in the memories of Orthodox Christians, and in spite of the fact that the excesses of the crusaders were deplored by Rome, the Latins were subsequently considered bitter enemies by both Greeks and Russians. Moreover, the Western neighbors who frequently attempted to invade Russia were Roman Catholics. The Swedes, the Teutonic Knights, the Poles, and the Lithuanians, all bearers of the Latin cross, constantly threatened Russia's borders. This threat hung over Russia throughout the centuries. When, in the seventeenth century, Demetrius, pretender to the throne of Moscow, seized the capital with the help of the Poles, he was accompanied by Jesuits and brought with him a Roman Catholic wife. A second false Demetrius also behaved as a usurper and an invader ; he too was supported by Poles, and this new outrage deepened the people's resentment and aggravated their hostility towards everything that emanated from the West. Even the Greek clergy who took refuge in Rome after the fall of Constantinople were suspected of Latin heresy.

How deep the distrust felt by the Russians towards Latinism actually was, is evidenced by the record which the Orthodox prelate Makarius [3] has preserved in his history of the Russian church. Makarius tells us that the Orthodox hierarchy of the sixteenth century drew up a list of "twenty-seven Latin errors." It attributed to the Roman Catholics "heresies of which the latter were actually entirely free," some of these "errors being quite insignificant and having nothing to do with faith." The list to which he refers is indeed confusing, for it presents, side by side, profound dogmatic differences (such as the teachings

[3] Makarius, *Istoria Russkoi Tzerkvi*, tome XI.

concerning the procession of the Holy Ghost, the primacy of the Pope, and Purgatory) and differences in ritual and even in customs. For example, Roman Catholics are accused of heresy for performing baptism by the sprinkling on of water instead of by immersion, for using unleavened bread in the Holy Sacrifice, for the observance of the Julian calendar, for fasting on Saturdays, for eating eggs and cheese during Lent, for prescribing celibacy to the priesthood, and so forth.

"The Russians," writes Makarius, "did not possess true and precise information concerning the errors of the Roman church; they multiplied their number, exaggerated the importance of many of them, believed all that was said . . . and were thus convinced that the Latins were the worst of all heretics, and that their heresy contained all the other heresies. The hatred of the Poles, bred by historical circumstances, confirmed them only more in this prejudice." [4]

Moscow felt secure only in her own faith, and since the Christianity of the West had been carried to Russia by corrupt representatives, every spiritual infiltration from the outside world was considered a corruption. This attitude gave the Russian church of that time its two dominant characteristics: a rigid conservatism in the carrying out of ritual, every word and gesture being considered an integral part of the Christian heritage, and a vivid consciousness of a great mission bestowed upon the Russian people to preserve true Christianity—a special design of God concerning them. This messianism was later developed by modern Russian thinkers of the Slavophile school.

In the sixteenth century, the Russian church had attained maturity. It was entirely independent of Byzantium and from 1589 was headed by its own patriarch. But in order to fulfil its mission and preserve the Christian heritage, it had to depend more and more on the support of the secular power. From

[4] *Ibid.*

Byzantium, Russia had received an organization which closely bound religion to the state. This affiliation now began to weigh on the church's destiny.

Joseph Sanin, founder and abbot of the Volokolamsk Monastery, was chiefly instrumental in bringing the church under the sway of the secular power. We have previously referred to this distinguished religious as one who furthered the development of the monasteries as economic units. He encouraged gifts and endowments; donations made in order to ensure continual prayers for the departed were among his chief sources of revenue; his estates were large and prosperous, and he administered them with a great deal of prudence and practical common sense. But the growth of these wealthy estates as rival economic powers disturbed the Moscow rulers. Prince Vassily even contemplated measures for the secularization of monastic property. Joseph sought a compromise: The prince needed the support of the church in state affairs and in his private life also, since his wife was childless and he wanted a divorce in order to remarry. Although the church opposed his remarriage, Joseph offered Vassily the support of his prestige, asking in return, the safeguard of his monastery's property. He was also ready to champion a close collaboration between the church and the secular power, with the understanding that the latter would not interfere with the black-cassock aristocracy.

In this policy Joseph manifested the prudence and practical gifts which had rendered the management of his community so efficient. He said himself that he applied in his negotiations a "godly-wise and God-inspired cunning." Russian historians consider him the founder of a strong state church. Indeed, after the time of Joseph the princedom of Moscow took the form of a theocracy in which church and state were closely united, the state safeguarding and forwarding the interests of the church so long as the church supported and obeyed the state. They held in common the concept of a "Third Rome."

Under Vassily's successor, John III, this concept was reinforced and took definite form. The prince added further distinction to the ruling family by marrying Sophia Paleologue, the daughter of the Byzantine emperor. He adopted Byzantine court etiquette, and the Byzantine two-headed eagle became the emblem of the Muscovite state. John III assumed the title of tsar, placing himself on an equal footing with the other European sovereigns. The prince of Moscow was by now an independent monarch who defied the remnants of the Mongol hordes and broke the last "straps of their yoke." In 1480 the Mongols withdrew from Russia without fighting, and those who remained were slain. A hundred years after Kulikovo, Moscow had attained her majority among European states.

It may seem as if this rapid development of church and state as coordinated powers would give inadequate scope to the growth of the contemplative life of the Seekers of Silence. Yet the spirit of the *thebaides* was still alive, and it revealed itself in the person of Joseph's contemporary and opponent, Nilus of Sorsk. Nilus was a monk of the Kirillov Monastery situated in Sorsk, beyond the Volga. He was a great mystic and ascetic, but like most of Russia's great religious teachers, he prescribed the "middle way of soberness." He, too, was the exponent of the kenotic spirit and of holy poverty: "Empty your cell," he counseled his brethren, "and the scarcity of things will inspire you with the spirit of abstinence." He was the originator of the so-called *skits,* which were small communities consisting of two or three monks living apart from the monastery and withdrawn from its commerce with the public, yet not entirely severed from it or committed to the rigors of the solitary life. *Skits* were later created in connection with many Russian monasteries, and the Startzy often withdrew to them.

Nilus of Sorsk visited the famous Greek monastery of Mount Athos and brought back a profound mystical teaching of a way to contemplation attained by a special spiritual exercise. The latter he called "mental doing" (or "doing of the heart"). It consisted of rhythmical breathing accompanied by the mental repetition of the ejaculation: "Lord Jesus Christ, forgive me," known in the Orthodox Church as the Prayer of Jesus. This method is based on the theory that in order to attain the state of contemplation man must render his mind deaf and dumb. He must safeguard his heart from all passions and preoccupations and control his very breathing, the beating of his heart, and the flow of his blood. He will then behold the "uncreated light of Mount Thabor." He will experience "ineffable joy," his tongue will be silent, prayer will fade from his lips, and "the mind, guide of our emotions," will lose its power. "Then," Nilus concludes, "the mind prayeth no more; it is lifted above prayer." [5]

A controversy between Nilus and Joseph broke out when the powerful abbot of Volokolamsk sought to dissolve certain heretical sects by inflicting imprisonment and capital punishment on their members. Nilus did not believe that heretics should be put to death or imprisoned, for "to judge either the just or the unjust and to banish or incarcerate them is no concern of the church." The church should use persuasion and prayer. Nilus and his followers, who were called the "Trans-Volga Elders," further sought to reestablish the true Christian spirit through the teaching and practice of poverty. In the eyes of these unworldly mystics who described themselves as "non-covetors" and "non-possessors" and who taught that monks should give all their possessions to the poor, Joseph and his disciples (the Josephites) were too much concerned with earthly goods.

Joseph and Nilus met at the church council of 1503. They opposed each other with vehemence. Nilus accused the "covet-

[5] There is a deep similarity between Nilus's spiritual exercises and the methods used by Western mystics such as St. John of the Cross, though the rhythmical breathing and control of heart and circulation seem to have had an Eastern origin. The expressions "mental doing" and "doing of the heart" are approximate translations of the Russian expressions. Soloviev describes the phenomenon as "mental operation," but that term seems to us too mechanical and rationalistic.

ous monks" of living "in a turmoil" and of having degraded religious life. Joseph objected that "without property there will be no honest and dignified communities." The council sided with Joseph, and Nilus's ideal of complete poverty was rejected. However, the controversy continued until the end of the sixteenth century. Nilus died long before it was over. During his lifetime, he refused all honors, and he asked to be buried "ignominiously." Since he forbade his monks to mention him in their chronicles, there is no document concerning him, and the circumstances of his life are known only from oral tradition.

Joseph died at the height of his prestige, respected by all his contemporaries. Despite the compromise which he had effected, he experienced some difficulty in maintaining his rights of property. The state, as we have seen, had entertained the plan of secularizing church possessions. In that Nilus had declared himself "non-covetous" he was regarded with a certain favor by the secular power. A law was introduced forbidding the church to increase its estates, to receive endowments securing prayers for the departed, and to buy land from laymen. This law was inspired by the non-covetors, who pursued their ends after Nilus's death.

But it was Joseph who triumphed in the long run. He was the actual founder of Muscovite theocracy based on a strong national church enjoying wealth and political influence yet obeying the tsar's wishes and defending the interests of the state (often at the expense of spiritual freedom). Nevertheless it cannot be said that Joseph was a mediocre religious and that Nilus alone embodied all that was good. That would be simplifying matters too much. While Nilus was seeking to produce spiritual men, Joseph was rebuilding a church which had been profoundly shaken by the Mongol invasion and which was to face many a fresh ordeal in the near future. It would be more just to say that both were outstanding personalities of their time, the exponents of two distinct currents of Russian religious life. Actually, the Russian church has canonized both Joseph of Volokolamsk and Nilus of Sorsk.

In spite of all its power and external magnificence, the state religion introduced by Joseph did not eclipse the inner man preached by Nilus, whose ideals lived on in the Russian people's soul. The deep kenotic current of Russian mysticism produced many saints, assumed many forms of religious experience. Even when its stream seemed to have dried up, hidden springs welled underground; they were to rise to the surface again in the nineteenth and twentieth centuries to give direction to a great religious and social movement. Whatever the vicissitudes of the official church, the spirit of the Seekers of Silence retained its integrity throughout the tragic and stormy episodes of Russian history.

IV

Moscow, the Third Rome

THE RIURIKOVITCH DYNASTY ended tragically. John IV, known as "the Terrible," killed his eldest son in a fit of insane rage and the little prince Dmitry was assassinated by the tsar's enemies. The heir to the throne, Fedor, died childless after a short reign, and Boris Godunov, a highly gifted statesman who had been Fedor's closest adviser, was elected tsar. There followed a period of interreign, bitter civil strife, and foreign wars known as the "troubled times." During this period two pretenders arose who successively attempted to identify themselves as the slain prince Dmitry, spreading the rumor that he had escaped his assassins and claiming his throne. Both usurpers were supported by the Poles, a circumstance which, as we have already pointed out, stimulated anti-Catholic feeling in Russia.

Moscow was seized by the Poles, who imprisoned Patriarch Germogen and let him die of starvation. Russia was in chaos, and it seemed as if the powerful Muscovite state had crumbled. It was only as the consequence of a deep surge of patriotism that the Russian people rallied under the leadership of the merchant Kuzma Minin and Prince Dmitry Pojarsky, supported by the ecclesiastical hierarchy. Once again, as in the days of the Mongols, church and state were in mortal danger and the peril was averted by the strong spiritual forces which were constantly shaping Russian unity. Moscow was liberated and the enemy expelled from Russian territory.

In 1612 a young boyar, Michael Romanov, was elected tsar. Although he belonged to the old Moscow nobility, he was

37

not the descendant of any of the princes who had been influential under the previous dynasty. He was the son of Patriarch Philarete, a great prelate and a wise and prudent statesman who had succeeded Germogen and played a prominent part in Russia's liberation. During his son's reign, the patriarch was the actual ruler of Russia. Under Michael Romanov and his successor, Alexis Mikhailovitch, Russia enjoyed national prosperity and spiritual growth. It was the beginning of a new era in Russian history which was to prepare the way for the creation of the empire of Peter the Great. During this period the Third Rome, which for many centuries had been severed from the rest of Europe, once more opened her doors to Western influences.

The initiation to Western civilization came gradually and in various forms. Many foreigners arrived in Moscow at that time. For the most part the newcomers were specialists and technicians called by the Romanovs to strengthen Moscow's military defense. Though the tsars greatly needed the help of these experts, the wave of xenophobia awakened during the "troubled times" had gathered force rather than subsided, and the foreigners were isolated in a Moscow suburb and kept under strict surveillance. There was a constant fear of alien influences and of the infiltration of Catholic missionaries or Protestant teachers; all foreign clerics were denied entrance to the country and any Russians who showed inclinations towards Catholicism or Protestantism were persecuted, imprisoned, or sent as penitents to secluded monasteries. Nevertheless Western spiritual and cultural influences were already beginning to make themselves felt.

Russian history is usually divided into two distinct periods: before and after Peter the Great. Before Peter the Great, there was ancient Muscovia, a mere reproduction of static Byzantine theocracy, a world in itself, completely isolated from the West. Peter the Great put an end to this isolation, "opened a window on Europe," and turned Russia into a great modern empire.

Although it cannot be denied that Russia underwent a deep transformation owing to the genius of Peter the Great, the transformation had actually begun long before Peter ascended the throne. Even under Alexis Mikhailovitch, a typical Muscovite tsar clothed in Byzantine robes, seventeenth century Russia was ripe for the great metamorphosis.

The immovable stronghold of the Third Rome ideology itself was gradually yielding to disintegrating influences from without. Russia's neighbor Poland played the part of a transmitting agent through which Russia received the first elements of Western culture. In spite of the ancient military hostility between them and Russia's distrust of Poland ingendered by Poland's interference with Russia's internal politics, Russia and Poland were sister nations; their blood would sometimes be aroused to throw them into bitter conflict with each other; but again the characteristics which they had in common would cause them to undergo similar reactions to European events. Since Poland had never partaken of Russia's rigid isolation from Western Europe, she was constantly subject to the impacts of change, and it was inevitable that some of the forces thus generated should have been conducted to Russia.

Perhaps Russia sometimes received these stimuli reluctantly. She was aware that like most spiritual forces they brought unrest and troubled her way of life. Moreover, Poland was not only the land of "Latin heresy"; she was also absorbing the spirit of the Reformation. The Protestant currents which were strong in Poland and Lithuania at that time penetrated into Russia and determined the creation of evangelical sects which have survived until today.

If Russia did not experience the direct impact of the Reformation, she did not entirely escape the consequences of the great spiritual crisis which shook Europe. For example, there was what the Russian historian Klyuchevsky calls "the Russian sixteenth century heretic of Protestant hue whose thought fed on doubts concerning dogma and ritual and who was a distant

echo of the storm of the Western reformation." There was
also the "Latinized" Russian nobleman, a product of west-
Russian influences or perhaps a pupil of Polish teachers, like
Prince Khvorostinine, a young man of old Moscow stock who
had been "infected with Catholic opinions" at the court of the
false Dmitry at a time when part of the Russian aristocracy
was in submission to the pretender's rule.

Under the Romanovs Khvorostinine was accused of subversive ideas and banished to a monastery. Later he obtained
pardon and returned to Moscow, professing a mixture of free
thought and confused Catholic and Protestant ideas. He attacked both the Orthodox faith and the Orthodox tsar, whom
he called the Russian despot. He wrote Latin verse and left
curious memoirs in which he bitterly criticized the laws and
customs of his country. Eventually, he was once more interned
in a monastery, where the monks tried in vain to make him
repent of his errors before his death. Prince Khvorostinine is
typical of his time. And he is also the distant and confused
precursor of a line of Russian thinkers in revolt against their
country's traditions. The first of these dramatic figures, he
seems to mark the first breach in the Third Rome's theocratic
stronghold.

During the reign of the first Romanovs, learned monks from
the Kiev Divine Academy were called to Moscow to spread
enlightenment. Although these scholars were devout members
of the Orthodox Church, their thinking had become imbued
with Western science and theology, for Kiev was nearer than
Moscow to Western Europe. Some of them had even visited
foreign countries and studied in Rome. They would go so far as
to adopt Catholicism temporarily in order to enter Catholic
seminaries, then return to Russia, where they would go back
to Orthodoxy, retaining the fruits of Western erudition.

There were highly cultured Moscow noblemen, "enlightened
boyars," who followed Western trends of thought and even

adopted the Western way of life. Prince Galitzine, who played an important part in state affairs and even held the reins of government at one time, introduced European customs in his home, decorated with foreign pictures and furniture. He wrote Latin verse, was tolerant towards the Western faith, and contemplated liberal reforms leading to the Europeanization of Russia. Tsar Alexis' chancellor and minister of foreign affairs, Afanassy Ordin-Nastchekin, a remarkable statesman and diplomat, actually foresaw and prepared the way for most of Peter's great reforms. He went even further, evolving the plan of a Slav federation headed by Russia and Poland which was to bring about the reconciliation of the sister nations.

But the most attractive of these "enlightened boyars" was Tsar Alexis' majordomo, Fedor Rtistchev, whom his contemporaries called *Milostivy Muj* ("Merciful Man"). Because of his great modesty, he often passed unnoticed among the more brilliant courtiers. Summing up Rtistchev's character, Russia's great historian Professor Klyuchevsky writes: "Out of the Gospel commandment: love thy neighbor as thyself, Rtistchev retained only the first part. He did not love himself . . . he was an entirely evangelical man, who turned his right cheek to him who had struck him on the left, as if obeying a mere physical law and not fulfiling a high feat of humanity." [1] Rtistchev did not know the feeling of resentment and revenge. A friend of whom he had been the benefactor turned against him and became his bitter enemy. Rtistchev regularly visited this man, seeking to regain his friendship. He would gently knock at the door and would be refused admittance; but he would return again and again. Finally the man let him in and began to abuse him, but Rtistchev only smiled and retired without a word of rebuke. When his enemy died he attended the funeral and seemed greatly moved.

Rtistchev accompanied Tsar Alexis on his military campaigns. During the course of these journeys he made himself

[1] Klyuchevsky, Vol. III.

responsible for the sick and wounded, whom he would lift into his carriage and bring to his own quarters to be tended. He distributed his land and riches to the poor, founded a hospital where not only invalids but drunkards were hospitalized, took care of criminals sent to jail, paid the ransoms of prisoners of war, fed the victims of famine. In his will, he instructed his heirs to treat his serfs kindly, "for they too are our brothers." He has gone down in Russian history as the first founder of charitable institutions.

Rtistchev was a highly cultured, and even a learned, man. Although a firm adherent of the Orthodox Church, he was open minded and tolerant. He enthusiastically advocated the study of Western science and founded a school of theology directed by the Kiev monks. In his personality there is presented a happy blending of what was best in the religion and culture of the old Russia with that new spirit which was leading Russia towards Europeanization. He was Tsar Alexis' closest friend and collaborator. There were among the enlightened boyars men more powerful than he, such as Morozov, who also furthered the spread of European culture and in his private life exchanged the rigid traditionalism of the old Moscow aristocracy for European ways, but despite his retiring nature, Rtistchev played an important part in the tsar's court. Although he refused all honors and distinctions, his contribution is not to be underestimated among the factors which rendered the period of Alexis' reign one of the most peaceful and harmonious in Russian history.

The Russian critic and historian Prince D. Mirsky describes Tsar Alexis as a "peace- beauty- and sport-loving monarch," whom his people called *Tishaishy* ("most quiet and peaceful"). "Certain aspects of Orthodoxy, not its most purely spiritual, but its æsthetic and humanistic aspects, found in him their most complete expression," Mirsky writes: "The essence of Alexis' personality is a certain spiritual epicurianism. It finds its expression in a firmly optimistic Christian faith, in a profound but unfanatical attachment to the sacred traditions and stately rituals of the Church, in a desire to see everyone around him happy and at peace, and in a highly developed capacity to extract a quiet and mellow enjoyment out of all things." [2]

However, there seems to have been something more than "spiritual epicurianism" at work in the atmosphere which pervaded Moscow in those days. The very fact that such men as Ordin-Nastchekin, Morozov, and Rtistchev appeared in Moscow's court circles is a proof that deeper and more creative energies were making themselves felt and that Russia was ripe for the great transformation which was to be effected by Peter the Great.

This ripening was indeed a harmonious and peaceful process. If it had been allowed to reach full development at its natural pace, Russia would have been spared the violent revolution from above effected by Peter. It is still a subject of heated discussions in Russian cultural circles whether Peter's reforms were not acts of unnecessary brutality, representing the forced implantation of Western techniques without consideration for Russia's authentic spirit. We shall have further occasion to refer to this issue, which formed the nucleus of most of the subsequent controversies of Russian thinkers. In the nineteenth century two intellectual currents were formed in Russia, the school of the Westerners, who defended Peter's Europeanization of Russia and the school of the Slavophiles, who criticized his reforms and adhered tenaciously to old Russian or Slav traditions.

For the present, let us cast a last glance at Moscow, the Third Rome, just as she is about to fade away: with her "most quiet" Tsar; her magnificent Byzantine court; her enlightened boyars; her foreign district full of German, Dutch, French, English, and Scandinavian technicians who will soon become the companions and advisers of young Tsar Peter; and last

[2] Mirsky, *A History of Russian Literature*, p. 37.

but not least, with her new political consciousness born during "the troubled times."

An important factor of the political life of this period was the so-called National Council, which was formed by representatives of the upper classes to decide upon important matters of state. The Romanov dynasty was itself an elected dynasty. It had been chosen by such a National Council, that is, by an assembly consisting of the princes, the military leaders, the clergy, the merchants—all those patriots who had saved Russia from foreign invasion and civil war. The Muscovite throne was still the stronghold of national and religious unity. The Muscovite rulers were still the lords of a theocratic state, conscious of a mission and jealously guarding the true faith. And yet, this new dynasty no longer represented power transmitted by right of succession. It was a new authority derived from the nation as a whole and regulated by a national assembly. And the tsar ceased to be what he had been in the days of Kalita, the landlord of an estate. He was now the head of a great and complex state machine for the good management of which he was responsible. He was the servant of the nation which had elected him.

This new concept of power was to be inherited and developed by Peter the Great. Russia was gradually emerging from Byzantine rigidity and turning Westward to seek a synthesis between the ancient traditions which she had outgrown and the modern European world.

V

The Raskol

MOSCOW'S HARMONIOUS EVOLUTION was troubled by a deep spiritual upheaval which rent the church with discord and created bitter conflict among the masses. Its repercussions lasted long after the death of Tsar Alexis; they continued to be felt under Peter the Great and his successors and its echoes are still alive in the Russia of today. This crisis is known in Russian history as the *Raskol*, or "inner schism," although the term is incorrect since the conflict was never concerned with dogma but was confined to questions of liturgy and custom in no way touching upon the essence of the Orthodox faith.

The occasion of this discord was the effort of the patriarch, Nikon, to make available to the Russian church the products of Greek erudition, from the sources of which Russian Orthodoxy had been separated by a series of historical accidents.

As we have seen, Russia had, from the very beginning, developed her own traditions, her own spiritual idiom, quite apart from the Byzantine mother church. Russian monks had not, for the most part, been scholars but had been educated in a tradition of piety which distrusted learning and considered science and rhetoric the manifestations of worldliness. The fall of Constantinople in 1453, which the Russian Orthodox had regarded as nothing more than retributive justice after the Florentine Union, had accentuated the estrangement between the Russians and the Greeks. Although the Greek ecclesiastical hierarchy had survived the Turkish onslaught, it was thought to have been "obscured" and "corrupted" by its intercourse

with the West. Moscow no longer recognized the authority of
the Greeks, regarding them with almost as much suspicion as
she regarded the Latins. Thenceforth, Russian Orthodoxy as a
whole had developed in strict accordance with national traditions. It is true that in the Divine Academy at Kiev, cultured
monks had remained open to both Eastern and Western currents and that the Romanovs had endeavored to introduce this
learning to Moscow, but the cultured monks were regarded
with hostility by their less scholarly co-religionists, and the influence which they were able to exercise on the Russian church
was inconsiderable.

Russia's isolation had been the cause of many distortions in
her religious culture. There had been inaccurate translations,
misinterpretations of texts, and errors in printing. Ikon painting had erred from the pure liturgical tradition, and certain
rituals, such as the manner of making the sign of the cross (the
Russians made it with two fingers instead of with three) and
that of singing the Alleluia had departed from the forms of the
Byzantine mother church. Of all this Patriarch Nikon was
justly aware, and not Nikon alone but other men of his time,
who saw the direction in which Russian Orthodoxy had been
drifting. The tsar's close adviser, Simeon Polotsky, who supported Nikon in his reforms, publicly declared that in all Russia
wisdom had no place to lay its head.

What Nikon desired was to draw the Russian church out of
its extreme nationalism, which had finally become provincial-
ism; to reestablish contact with the learned monks and the
scholarly and artistic tradition of the Greek church; to gain
access to the cultural advantages of Western Europe. Like the
tsar, like Rtistchev and his friends, the patriarch was interested
in furthering the accomplishments of the Kiev academy. His
aims were amply justified in themselves, but in their accom-
plishment he encountered two main obstacles: the form which
the Third Rome tradition had taken in the Russian church
and the inflexibility of his own nature. A man of broad vision

and unquestionably high motives, he was nevertheless unable to make to opponents of equally unquestionable sincerity the concessions which would have secured their cooperation.

We have observed how liturgy and custom had become identified with dogma in the Russian religious consciousness. It had been through ritual and religious art, not through theological teachings, that the masses had absorbed the principles of the Christian faith. With the passing of the years, the liturgical tradition of the Russian Orthodox Church had assumed absolute importance in the minds of the people. Not a word, not a sign or a symbol could be altered without gravely imperilling the sacred truth of which the Russian church was now the only true bearer. Inevitably, the correction of the sacred books and the revision of the liturgy provoked impassioned opposition. Acquiescence on the part of conservative Russians was made all the more difficult by the fact that Nikon had to appeal to the Greek ecclesiastical authority for assistance in the work of correction.

With the help of Greeks and Ukrainians, Nikon pursued the revision. And because he sought the aid of foreigners and of foreign-minded members of the Orthodox Church he awakened the suspicion of the people and their pastors. "Forget the Kyrie Eleison of the Hellenes," wrote Archpriest Avvakum to the tsar, "and defy them Thou art the son of Michael, a Russian, and not a Greek. Speak the native tongue. Do not debase it. . . . The Lord has the same love for us as he has for the Greeks. Through Cyrill and Methodius he gave us the reading and writing in our tongue. What could we have better than this, unless it be the tongue of the angels?"

Nikon was accused of eating and dressing like a Greek, of despising the Russian way of life, of favoring aliens. And if Greek influences had awakened suspicion, the Latin infiltrations fully aroused it. There was a rumor that Nikon was surrounded by men of "obscure Roman errings," by priests who had studied in Catholic seminaries or were of Polish background. The sophisticated Kiev monks irritated the priests of Moscow. Clouds of distrust and resentment gathered, but it was the drastic measures which Nikon took to quell opposition that precipitated the storm.

A peasant's son and thus a "self-made" man, Nikon had risen from the status of an obscure monk, to move in the highest ecclesiastical circles. He was an administrator of great energy and erudition, who held that a strong church was one ruled by iron hierarchical discipline. When his opponents accused him of wanting to imitate the methods of the Catholic Church, he would reply, "Well, the Pope also is right in some of the things he does! In Rome they are ruled by St. Peter and St. Paul!" Unfortunately, he was not content to apply such authority as he legitimately possessed but gave vent to his imperious and wilful temper. When part of the clergy objected to his reforms, he threw them into prison, exiled them, put them into chains, or burned them at the stake. His opponents, the *Raskolniki* ("Dissidents"), called him a heretic and refused to be subject to him.

Among the men whom Nikon turned against him were a group of distinguished priests, the so-called "Zealots of Faith": There was Stefan Vonifatiev, who had been the tsar's confessor; the preachers Neverov and Longin; the famous Archpriest Avvakum, one of the most colorful figures of his time. Before the schism these priests had striven for the purification of Russian morals, denouncing the drinking bouts and loose living of the boyars, the ignorance of the clergy, the debauchery of the common people. They had started a religious revival in Moscow and had enjoyed the favor of the tsar, of Rtistchev, and of Nikon himself, who had been their intimate friend.[1]

When the Zealots of Faith joined the Raskol and rose against Nikon, the state church lost its most gifted pastors and the

---

[1] The French scholar Pierre Pascal, who made intensive research into the Raskol, compared the Russian Zealots of Faith with the French Jansenists. See Pascal, *Avvakum et les Debuts du Raskol.*

Raskol became invested with the highest moral authority. Had Nikon temporized and accomplished his reforms by persuasion, he would have brought them back. Instead, he inflicted the most unremitting persecution upon them, thus turning them into martyrs. Nikon's successors used the same methods, with the same results. The clergy and the people were split into factions, and a constant source of spiritual, and even political, unrest was created. The Raskolniki, or the "Old Believers," as they were also called, were solemnly anathematized. This meant that millions of the members of the Orthodox Church were excommunicated and left without attachment to any ecclesiastical body.[2]

The Raskol is one of the most dramatic pages in the history of the Russian church. Although at first it appeared to be the reaction of conservatism, it rapidly developed into a powerful stream of rebellion—rebellion against the Josephite state church supported by the secular arm, against Greek scholasticism—in fact, against all the established institutions and traditions. If we are to understand the violence of this protest, we must recall that to the Russian people the concept of the Third Rome had become an article of faith. When the reforms were supported by the tsar himself the masses were convinced that the church was passing from the earth and that the end of the world must be at hand. In the person of the tsar they beheld none other than the Antichrist whose coming had been prophesied. Thus the church and the state had failed the people at the same time, and this spiritual shock elicited in its intensity the extremist tendency which the contemplatives had constantly sought to correct by the cultivation of the middle way of spiritual sobriety.

As the Raskol spread through Russia it split into two groups, one of which was still led by priests ordained by the Orthodox

[2] This measure was later abrogated, and the Raskolniki are no longer considered outside the Orthodox Church, although they still form a separate branch of it and there is no intercourse between them and the official Russian clergy.

Church and the other of which would no longer accept the "corrupted" church as an intermediary but chose to go without priests or sacraments, calling itself "the priestless."

The belief that the end of the world was at hand produced in the most radical of the dissidents a kind of ecstatic tension which, in its most violent manifestations, assumed the form of a thirst for martyrdom. The old ideal of nonresistance to force found expression in those who welcomed persecution. And there were those who, seeking to anticipate the ultimate purgation by fire and water, burned themselves alive or drowned themselves.

The less radical among the Raskolniki were no less distrustful of the world, and so they withdrew from it. Raskolnik monks took refuge in the great Solovetzk Abbey on the White Sea, which was besieged by Nikon's soldiers. Agricultural communities were formed in the wilderness, like those of the Seekers of Silence. And there were "wanderers in Christ," who preached the most extreme doctrines, disavowing not only the official church but also the state, war, taxes, legal marriage, the written law, and every kind of oath. Both the negation of juridical forms and the tendency towards a communal life in radical detachment from established patterns are very typical of Russian social aspirations carried to the extreme. In their elemental, anarchical protest, the Raskolniki can be considered the precursors of the Russian revolutionists of the twentieth century.

When Nikon began his controversy with the Raskolniki he did not consider them heretics. To the preacher Ivan Neverov, who was one of the champions of the Raskol, he said that both "old and new [corrected] books" were good and could be used indiscriminately. Historians stress the fact that the patriarch imposed penalties not on the attachment to the old books but on rebellion. It was only as a consequence of his imperious behaviour and the resentment of his opponents that the rift had become irreparable.

Nikon's indisputable merit is to have saved the Russian church from particularism. Had it not been for him, Muscovite Orthodoxy would have completely drifted from its original sources, becoming a provincial faith entirely cut off from the universal stream of Christian culture. But his ruthless methods entirely missed their aim. His opponents represented an immense potential of spiritual energies of which the patriarch's intemperance deprived the church, thus undermining its foundation. Nor did he succeed in maintaining his own authority for long. His imperious character and inflexible behavior gained him numerous and powerful enemies, eventually alienating even Tsar Alexis. When Nikon was finally condemned and deposed, he left a church profoundly shaken and weakened. Its influence had considerably decreased among the masses, and the monarch had ceased to fear its sanctions. This facilitated the task of Peter the Great, who less than half a century later suppressed the patriarchate and secularized Russia.

As a result of the Raskol many outstanding personalities made their appearance. The most interesting is Archpriest Avvakum, of whose sufferings we have an intimate record in his autobiography. As we have seen, he was one of the Zealots of Faith. The son of a village priest of Nijny Novgorod, he was known for his austere life and high moral standards. His zeal held his parishioners in fear and trembling until one day they rose against him and beat him. This was the prelude to his innumerable tribulations.

Avvakum's fame as a preacher had spread throughout Moscow before the schism. The tsar had favored him. He had been a friend of Fedor Rtistchev and an intimate of Nikon, but when he joined the Raskol with the other Zealots, he suffered the most bitter persecution at the hands of the patriarch. He was thrown into prison and put into chains. Yet he did not lose courage, and he received great spiritual consolations. As he writes in his *Life,* an angel visited him in prison, bringing

him bread and cabbage soup. Later, he was released and
banished with his wife to Siberia, whither he journeyed as
chaplain to the expeditionary force of Pashkov, a military
commander who was engaged in the conquest of the Daur
region (Transbaikalia). Pashkov treated his chaplain more
like a prisoner than a minister of God. He bullied and brutal-
ized him, half drowned him, and tried to make him perform
a mock marriage. When the priest refused, the general abandoned him in the Siberian wilderness.

Describing his experience in his *Life,* Avvakum is not too
absorbed in his personal woes to present a detailed picture of
his surroundings. In spite of his fear and dismay, he retained,
as a true man of letters, an eye for the beauties of nature. From
his descriptions we learn something about Siberia's inexhaustible fauna:

Alackaday! the mountains were high, the ravines impassible,
there was a stone crag, that stood like a wall—you'd crick your
neck before you saw the top. In these mountains great serpants
were to be found and in them dwelt geese and ducks with read
feathers, and black crows and grey jackdaws; in these mountains
were also eagles and hawks and gerfalkons and guinea fowl and
swans and other wild things in plenty, every variety of bird.
Moreover on these mountains many wild beasts wandered at
liberty, wild goats, and deer, and bison, and elk, and boars and
wild sheep—clearly to be seen, but not to be caught.[4]

When Avvakum finally returned to Pashkov's forces, he was
thrown into a dungeon. During the following campaign he
nearly died of starvation and was often cruelly beaten.

"We must through much tribulation enter the kingdom of
God," Avvakum exclaimed, as the boat which he had boarded
began to sink. On another occasion he and Dame Avvakum
were pushed out of the sleigh in which they were riding into

[4] Harrison and Mirrlees, trans., *Life of Avaakum,* p. 64.

deep snow. They got up and painfully continued their way on foot:

"My poor woman tramped along, and at last she fell," writes the archpriest, who fell on top of her, crying: "Oh my dear lady, your pardon!" . . . "And the poor soul began to complain to me saying: 'How long, Archpriest, are these sufferings to last?' And I said: 'Till our death!' And she with a sigh answered: 'So be it, let us be getting on our way.' " [5]

There is both pathos and humor in Avvakum's autobiography. As the reader follows him through his prisons and into the Siberian wilderness, he sometimes cannot help smiling at the adventures of the Archpriest and Dame Avvakum. Yet the poor priest's ordeals were real enough. He was continually in danger of his life, and so was his long-suffering wife and the child she bore him during their three-thousand-mile journey from Moscow to Tobolsk. After having escaped innumerable perils, the Zealot took refuge in a remote village, where for nine years he continued to suffer persecution.

Avvakum was a stubborn man, fearless in the face of danger and sternly resolved to be a martyr to the old faith. As soon as he was allowed to return to Moscow, he once more threw himself into the fray. Nikon had been deposed, but his successor compelled Avvakum to don a monk's habit and banished him to Pustozersk, in the extreme northeast of Russia, opposite the coast of Nova Zembla. But nothing could break his indomitable spirit. He was, as one of his biographers describes him, "a fiery fighter, a good hater and a good friend. Scorn and hatred are mixed in his writings with a fierce and manly tenderness." [6]

Avvakum's *Life* is indeed one of the masterpieces of Russian literature. He was the first Russian author to write in a realistic, direct style instead of imitating the flowery rhetoric of Byzantine pious works. There are many moving, tragic, and colorful

[5] *Ibid.,* p. 81.   [6] Mirsky, p. 42.

episodes in his autobiography. He describes himself, Dame Avvakum, his friends, disciples, and persecutors in a vivid language which recreates this dramatic scene in Russian history. Thanks to Avvakum, the period is still extraordinarily alive; we can still feel its pulsations. We behold the proud, inflexible Nikon, the rough, brutal Pashkov, the nonconformist Zealots of Faith and their fanatical followers.

And there is something more in Avvakum's *Life*: it is a mystical writing, the narrative of a man who was a poet and a visionary. When he describes the angel who visited him in jail to comfort him, he makes the heavenly messenger as real as if he had touched him with his own hands. If he scoffed at the scholars' rhetoric, at the learned men whom he called the "almanac-mongers," it is because he had the simple faith rooted in direct religious experience:

Of old the Devil did say: "I shall erect my throne in heaven and I shall be equal unto the Almighty." . . . And likewise do the almanac-mongers say: "We understand the things of heaven and earth, and who is equal unto us?" But what Christians achieve is not external wisdom, nor the understanding of the movements of the moon, but they mount to heaven itself by their humility, and their bodies remain incorrupt on earth. Look then, proud almanac-mongers, where are thy Pythagorases and Platos: they have all been eaten by worms. . . . But my saints for the sake of their humility, have been glorified by God.[7]

Avvakum was a man deeply strengthened by suffering and joyfully accepting it for Christ's sake. He was resolved to bear his tribulations till his death, as he had told Dame Avvakum.

To one of his disciples he wrote:

And even if they begin to scourge you and burn you, all the more glory to God for that! For this we come out of our mother's womb. You will not be very long burning in the fire—just the

[7] This and the following passage are quoted from Avvakum's epistle to a friend, translated by Prince D. Mirsky. See Mirsky, *op. cit.*, pp. 41–42.

twinkling of an eye—and the soul is free. Are you afraid of the furnace? Play the man, spit at it, do not be afraid! Fear comes before the fire; but once you are in it, you forget it all. You catch fire, and here they are, Christ and the host of angels with Him; they take the soul out of the body and carry it to Christ, and He, the good Lord, blesses it and fortifies it with divine force. It is no longer heavy, but becomes as though winged; it flies off in company with the angels; it hovers like a bird, glad to be free from its prison. . . . Be eager to sacrifice yourselves. My poor little Russians, glad they are to have found at last a tormentor: in legions do they leap into the fire. I would lief die, and then die again for the sake of Christ and God.

Avvakum preached martyrdom all his life, and he himself died at the stake. He was publicly burned with his two closest followers, Epiphanius and Lazarus.

VI

Yury Krijanitch

ON ONE OCCASION during the period when the exiled Avvakum was living in the city of Tobolsk, a scholar whose identity
was unknown to him came to his door. Although the man was a
Slav and spoke the Russian tongue fluently, Avvakum refused
him admittance, asking him suspiciously to what faith he
belonged. "I belong to the true apostolic faith," the stranger
replied, "so please let me enter your house." But as he gave no
further information, the stubborn Avvakum shut the door in
his face.

The visitor retired regretfully. He had been eager to meet
the famous Zealot and to discuss the Raskol. Although he was
reputed to be in sympathy with the patriarch's reforms, he
was nevertheless interested in the Old Believers' point of view.
He was highly trained in theology and in the various branches
of science. He was also an exile, but his position was less pain-
ful that that of Avvakum, since he was not harassed by the
administration but was being permitted to prepare a work of
erudition for the tsar himself. This man, who had arrived in
far-away Tobolsk after many adventures and ordeals, was
Yury Krijanitch, a Catholic priest from Croatia, whom historians recognize as one of the earliest exponents of panslavism.

Yury Krijanitch was born in 1610 in Zagreb. He studied in
Vienna, in Bologna, and in Rome, where he was admitted to
the College of St. Athanasius created by the Congregation de
Propaganda Fide in order to train missionaries for Slavonic
lands. After his graduation, he wrote a learned treatise entitled

OUR LADY OF THE SIGN. SS. NICHOLAS AND STEPHEN
THE GUIDE. AROUND 1600

Bibliotheca Schismaticorum. This work, which is still preserved in Rome at the library of St. Maria Sopra Minerva, gives clear indication of the extraordinary erudition of the young doctor who was awaiting his Congregation's permission to go as a missionary to Muscovia.

Krijanitch differed essentially from the Roman priests usually sent to evangelize Slavonic countries. To begin with, he did not think that evangalization was necessary. The Slavs were already Christians, and in spite of the Schism, bound to the Universal church by patristic tradition, the sacraments, and the apostolic succession, which they had preserved intact. They had adhered to the Byzantine schismatics because of historical circumstances and ignorance of the true elements of the conflict, Krijanitch believed. Therefore they were to be considered not schismatics but separated brothers. Moreover, being a Slav himself, Krijanitch was aware that the observance of the Eastern rite and the use of the Slavonic language were essential in Russian religious life. He stressed the importance of this fact and opposed all attempts to Latinize the Russian church. This point of view, which is clearly formulated for the first time in his doctoral treatise, was developed two and a half centuries later by Wladimir Soloviev, the great apostle of Union, and became the official doctrine of the Vatican.

In this, as in many other things, Krijanitch was a precursor. But more remarkable still is the fact that this humble priest who, after receiving his doctorate, became attached to an obscure Croat parish, had a precise, clear, and even prophetic, vision of Russia's destiny among the nations of the world.

Krijanitch had been drawn to Russia since his earliest youth. He had read all that had been written about Muscovia: the narratives of famous travellers such as Olearius, the reports and letters of legates and missionaries, and the works which had been written concerning controversial questions. He was aware of a deep organic tie still binding Russia to the religious world of the West. All that came from Muscovia was eagerly absorbed by him. In Vienna and in Rome he had talked to the Russian emissaries who occasionally visited the Western capitals. He knew everything that was going on in Moscow. He had heard about the enlightened boyars, about Fedor Rtistchev and St. Andrew's Monastery, which the latter had recently founded and where the Kiev Monks taught Greek and Latin. He was informed of Russia's state affairs and of her economic and cultural conditions. To him there seemed to be every indication that Russia had broken the rigid mould of Byzantine conservatism and that great dynamic forces were at work.

The young Croatian doctor developed his ideas and plans in a special report to the Congregation. The Muscovites, he stated once more, were not heretics. Since they had been separated from Rome as the result of ignorance, all that was required was to enlighten them. The Muscovites were to receive the benefit of education. They were to learn Greek and Latin and be initiated to the culture of western Europe. They were to improve their political and economic conditions. At the same time, they were to learn more about their own history and that of the other Slavonic nations. They would then become aware of the full possibilities of a broadened horizon which would unite them as a mother with all the Slavonic peoples and as a church with the peoples of the West. This original plan of uniting all Slavonic races under Moscow was later elaborated by Krijanitch in works which he wrote in Siberia, but the main outlines of his scheme and his concept of Russia's universal mission were clearly set forth long before he had crossed the Russian border. So fascinated was he by his vision of panslavism that he made an exhaustive study of all Slavonic languages, compiled a grammar, and sought to create a common idiom, a sort of Slavonic *esperanto,* by means of which all the peoples of his race should be able to understand one another.

The plan conceived by Krijanitch was bold, original, almost fantastic; yet it was based on sound erudition. Even today, scholars consider his linguistic research a remarkable piece of work, and his knowledge of Russia and of the intricacies of Orthodox religious trends satisfy the most exacting reader.

The Congregation studied his report attentively. It appreciated the quality of his scholarly research but frowned on the young priest's boldness. His request to go to Muscovia was left without an answer. No support was offered him for his projected journey. Instead of being "rushed" to Moscow, as he had expected, he was ordered to write a treatise concerning the schismatics.

Krijanitch possessed a great deal of enthusiasm and erudition but little patience. He was hot-tempered and stubborn. He would not hear of giving up his plan, but repeated his request. He wrote, expostulated, insisted that the Congregation examine his suggestions further. But still there was no answer. So he made one last desperate attempt to realize his scheme. He joined a foreign embassy en route for Moscow and arrived there disguised as an official attached to the mission.

This first visit to Russia did not yield any considerable results. It was difficult for a foreigner to make his way into exclusive Moscow circles. But it seems that he had an interview with the patriarch, and it is also probable that he called on Fedor Rtistchev, who was open-minded towards the Latins and more hospitable to strangers than the other Moscow noblemen. Krijanitch certainly met persons who were not hostile to Catholics. He even hinted in his report to the Congregation that he had been in touch with people in favor of union. It is difficult to ascertain to what extent these observations were correct. Father Pierling,[1] the learned Jesuit who has devoted exhaustive research to Catholicism in Russia, believes that there were in Moscow at that time a few "crypto-Catholics," that is, Russians professing Catholicism in secret.

[1] Pierling, *La Russie et le Saint Siège*.

Yury Krijanitch may have met some of them, but he appears to have overestimated the possibilities of union, as he was later to find out for himself.

Krijanitch's only achievement during that first journey to Moscow was the acquisition of a recent publication issued by the patriarch in order to combat Catholic and Protestant influences in Russia. This work, obtained at great cost and after many difficulties, contains a complete theological exposition of the questions at issue, treated from the Orthodox point of view. The occasion of its publication was the engagement of the tsar's daughter to a Danish Prince. The prince, who was a Protestant, arrived at Moscow accompanied by the Protestant minister attached to the Court of Denmark. When the tsar asked that his future son-in-law renounce Protestantism and become a member of the Orthodox church, the prince suggested that his pastor should discuss the matter with the Moscow clergy. There followed a series of debates which soon provoked bad feeling on both sides. The prince remained unconvinced and returned to Denmark without marrying the tsar's daughter. Thereupon the Moscow hierarchy decided it was the proper time to deal with all heretics, whether Protestant or Latin, and the theological treatise in question was composed by Orthodox scholars.

Once more Krijanitch settled down in Rome, still eyed with distrust by the Congregation, which considered his journey to Russia an act of disobedience. Nevertheless his work and the information he supplied were examined, and after many hesitations which tried his patience sorely, the Congregation officially allowed him to return Eastward. But new disappointments awaited him. He was sent not to Muscovia but to Galicia. Instead of being encouraged to study the rite of the Uniates, who belonged to the Eastern liturgical branch, he was attached to a Latin bishopric. The bishop was a harsh and imperious man who made Krijanitch recite the office instead of devoting himself to scholarly research. When the Croat protested, he was put under arrest. Finally, Krijanitch got into touch with a Uniate monastery and was invited to stay at the castle of a Uniate nobleman. But his further plans were already mapped out. Two months later he was on his way to Moscow.

Krijanitch journeyed through the Ukraine at a time when the country was rent by civil war. One part of the Cossacks was in alliance with Poland while the other supported Moscow. Krijanitch took an active interest in the struggle. Because he believed that destiny pointed to the union of all Slavonic peoples under the Russian tsar, he sided with Moscow, writing a proclamation in which he advised all the people to pledge allegiance to Alexis. Although a foreigner, Krijanitch knew more about the conflict and the issues at stake than did many a Cossack. His proclamation was publicly read and was used as propaganda for the Russian cause long after its author had left the Ukraine.

When Krijanitch arrived in Moscow in 1659, the Raskol had already swept Russia. The Croat had studied the problem as attentively as he had studied the Cossack conflict, and he immediately plunged into the fray. He believed in unity above all things, and he saw in Nikon the symbol of unity. Although he himself was a Catholic by birth and communion, he felt that Moscow's Orthodox Church stood for national strength and harmony as a corrective to the people's obscurantist and anarchical tendencies, so he sided with the church against the Raskolniki and wrote a treatise defending Nikon.

As soon as Krijanitch arrived in Moscow, he sent a request to the tsar, asking to be appointed court librarian. This post, he hoped, would permit him to undertake his mission of enlightenment. The offer of his services as librarian was rejected, but he was given a subsidy of three rubles a day and ordered to prepare a grammar and lexicon. Even this obscure position delighted the Croat, who now felt solid ground under his feet. It was as if he had come home after an endless search. "They call me a wanderer," he wrote. "This is not true. I have come to the Tsar of my race, to my own people, to the only country where my works can be utilized and do some good."

Krijanitch had still many illusions concerning his adopted fatherland. He was not at the end of his wanderings. A little more than a year after his arrival, his work was suddenly interrupted. The Moscow authorities became suspicious of this foreigner who, though he carefully disguised his identity, looked like a Catholic cleric. He was banished to Siberia. It is thus that he arrived in Tobolsk almost at the same time as Avvakum. But while the latter was treated harshly, Krijanitch was attached as official to the Tobolsk authorities. He was, moreover, allowed to go on with his scholarly work.

The champion of panslavism spent fifteen years as a exile in Siberia. The work he accomplished during that period of enforced tranquility is immense. He completed his grammar and lexicon, wrote a treatise on Siberia and its natural resources, corresponded with Western scholars and geographers, to whom he gave information concerning Russia's Asiatic empire. He devoted a study to the sacrament of baptism, which was one of the focal points of controversy between the Orthodox Church and the church of Rome. And he perfected his panslavonic language, which he intended to be used by all the peoples of his race. But his most important work during his Siberian exile was his *Politica,* which was followed by his *De Providentia Dei.* These two books summarize his ideas concerning Russia. Both works were written in the universal Slavonic language invented by Krijanitch, with occasional lapses into Latin. Nevertheless they are still quite readable, and even today they are far from being out-of-date. Russian scholars have devoted many an exhaustive study to them, and they have been incorporated into Russian culture.

In our day, the Croat's learned treatises would be called historiosophic studies, since they deal with Russia's historical destinies, her national psychology, her political trends, and her religious aspirations. It is a complete survey of seventeenth-century Muscovia, and it is also a glance into a future as glorious in the author's mind as that conceived by the ideologists of the Third Rome. The only difference is that Krijanitch beholds Russia gradually moving towards union with the West, whereas Orthodox writers wanted her to preserve the "pure faith" inherited from Byzantium. It can be said that most Russian thinkers, whether inclining towards Eastern or towards Western tradition, have something in common with Krijanitch in so far as they believe in Russia's special mission. This does not mean, however, that Krijanitch was satisfied with painting a glorious picture of the Muscovite empire of the future. He clearly saw the shortcomings of the empire of his day and wrote about them quite frankly: ignorance, administrative chaos, the exploitation of the Russian people by foreigners, and the government's arbitrary rule—such were the main evils afflicting Russia. But Krijanitch firmly believed that these evils were temporary. Russia had potentialities for greatness. He expressed the idea formulated in the West by Leibnitz, that the various nations succeed one another as the bearers of a universal good, and he stated that Russia was called to play a prominent role in the future civilized world.

As yet Muscovia was not ripe for her mission. She had first to learn from other countries; she had to put her inner affairs in order, to overcome her inertia and obscurantism, to regain her political balance.

"Our great misfortune," Krijanitch wrote, "is our lack of moderation in the exercise of power: we are unable to observe the middle way: we have no sense of measure. We go to extremes and wander on the brink of precipices!" These lines are a striking definition of Russian psychology. They express that peculiar maximalism which characterizes Russian rulers and Russian political trends beginning with Peter's drastic reform of the Russian state and ending with the Bolshevist revolution. The Russian is not afraid of the effort necessary to surmount obstacles or of "wandering on the brink of precipices," but he is afraid of all that is flat, uneventful, mediocre. He is afraid of the middle way. Having enumerated Moscow's defects, the author paints the magnificent future which awaits her when these evils are corrected. She will manifest her power and dynamism. She will unite all the Slavs under the tsar's sceptre, which he compares to "the staff of Moses."

Krijanitch gives a detailed description of Russia's natural resources and how they are to be used, together with a list of the economic and political reforms which he considers urgent. Though he believes in a centralized autocracy, he demands certain freedoms: the autonomy of merchants' guilds; the power of organization for artisan's corporations; protective legislation for peasant labor. He also stipulates some form of popular representation. Schools of arts and crafts with special branches for women are recommended. A bride, he believes, should be able to show her husband a good artisan's degree. The Russians should be technically trained. Foreign textbooks and technical works should be translated and distributed. Tradesmen should be taught arithmetic and bookkeeping. If they refuse to study, their stores should be closed until they have learned their lesson.

The work of Yury Krijanitch is not pure academic speculation. It is based on genuine experience and more than once it strikes a practical note. The author came to Russia with no desire to devote his life to research into the abstract. Rather did he come to hasten the transformation of the Moscow tsardom. How far did he achieve his goal?

His hopes of a Slavonic federation did not materialize, and his plans for immediate reform could not be carried out. He sent his *Politica* and his *De Providentia Dei* to the tsar, but received no reply. He begged for permission to return to Moscow, only to be informed that he would obtain pardon if he renounced his faith. He rejected the offer and remained in Tobolsk. It was only after Tsar Alexis' death that he was finally permitted to leave Siberia and settle down in the capital under the tsar's successor, Fedor. He was then allowed to live openly as a priest, but after his fifteen years of exile, the Moscow tsardom seemed like a prison, and he soon asked for a passport to return to the West.

For a long time, he was forbidden to leave Russia. It seemed as if throughout his life he had been subjected to delays with the result that he had lived in eternal expectation. Months elapsed before he was finally allowed to cross the border into Poland, where he retired to a Dominican monastery. From there, he sent the Congregation a detailed report of his adventures and his experience in Muscovia. His writings were carefully examined by a body of learned Jesuits, who declared that they were based on sound doctrine; nevertheless his Moscow mission was ended for good. Nor did he find peace of mind in his new surroundings. He was the eternal wanderer whom the "tsar of his race" had rejected. At last he set out for Rome in order to report personally to the Congregation, but he died on the way in besieged Vienna, where he acted as chaplain, tending the sick and wounded.

Meanwhile the *Politica* and the *Providentia Dei* lay in the archives of the Moscow palace. One day, young Tsar Peter discovered them "somewhere in the attic," as the historians tell us. Did he study the great scheme of Yury Krijanitch? It seems, at least, that in some of his reforms he followed the path indicated by the Croat, but how much Peter derived from the books remains a matter of supposition. However, Professor Klyuchevsky writes:

Reading the program of Krijanitch, we involuntarily exclaim: this is the program of Peter the Great! with its very defects and contradictions, with its faith in the creative force of the Ukaze and in the possibility of spreading education with the help of books translated from the German or through the closing of the store of a tradesman who refuses to learn arithmetic. . . .[2]

[2] Klyuchevsky, *op. cit.*

Like Peter the Great, Krijanitch saw beyond these technicalities. He was conscious of Russia's immense possibilities and was eager to hasten her growth because he was sure that she was able to yield her fruit. He was the first to ask himself: What is Russia's place in the civilized world? and to answer: She stands between the East and the West and must serve as a link between the two cultures. This essential theme of Russian historiosophy was to be developed in the nineteenth century by two great thinkers, Peter Chaadaiev and Wladimir Soloviev. After the Bolshevist revolution it was resumed by the Eurasian school, which has influenced modern Russian thought.

In the history of union, Yury Krijanitch also played the part of a precursor. He was the first Catholic scholar who grasped the intangible religious bond between East and West. Much of what he taught was ignored or misunderstood in his day. In the eyes of his contemporaries, his dogma appeared sound but his ideas seemed too bold and his zeal unbalanced by impatience. In Moscow he was an unwelcome guest; his erudition, the vastness of his schemes, struck fear to the hearts of the unlearned and aroused scepticism in the minds of scholars. It was considered safer to keep him out of mischief in faraway Siberia. Yet his views on the Schism, on Russia's religious destinies and political development, remain fundamentally sound and still offer food for thought. In Russian culture, Krijanitch stands on the very threshold of the new era. His dream of enlightenment and reform actually took shape. Russia under Peter the Great became the mighty empire of which he had conceived. It was the end of her political and spiritual isolation.

VII

From Peter to Pushkin

RUSSIA'S EXTRAORDINARY DEVELOPMENT consequent to the reforms of Peter the Great, who "opened a window on Europe," is considered almost miraculous. Like the magic plant of the Fakirs, the tree of the modern Russian Empire grew and blossomed in a few decades. In the eighteenth century, the formerly static Moscow tsardom became a great, full-fledged European power. Enlightenment came as a flash, but the very swiftness of the process was the cause of three of the principal defects in the society which it produced.

First, Russia did not take over the entire heritage of European culture which the continuity between the Middle Ages and the Rennaissance had made an organic whole. Without the preparation which the flowering of medieval culture had afforded European civilization, Russia was suddenly and almost violently stimulated by the intellectual currents emanating from modern Europe, such as Protestant rationalism and the writings of the French Encyclopaedists. This intellectualism animated the generation which was to have the most important part in the building of the new empire. Russia's "enlightened" noblemen became free thinkers, disciples of Voltaire.

Second, the link with Russia's past was brutally broken by Peter. He swept away old prejudices and conventions; in many respects he was a revolutionary and a non-conformist. But, as is the way with revolutionaries eager to create a new world, he stifled, or at least silenced for a long time the expression of Russia's spiritual and national genius. The severest blow was dealt to the church when he suppressed the patriarchate and instituted in its place a church administration of Protestant pattern, entirely subservient to the state. He thus weakened and chained down the forces which had built and cemented the Third Rome. This brutal suppression of the past left a gap in Russia's development. Men of the eighteenth, and especially of the nineteenth, century felt uprooted, vagrant; they drifted along tortuous paths of doubt and negation; or else they hastened to assert new values with a fanaticism untempered by the sober spirituality of a St. Sergius or a Nilus of Sorsk.

Third, enlightenment came to the upper classes, while the masses still lived in ignorance. Peter's reforms scarcely changed their lot. The tsars of Moscow had made them serfs. They were attached to the soil and their masters could dispose of them according to their whims and fancies. The landlord held their destiny in his hands; he dealt out rewards and punishments. And he was regularly obliged to furnish a contingent of these peasants to the tsar's army. Peter's reforms were mainly political, administrative, and fiscal. He did not ameliorate the social conditions of the masses. The peasants remained serfs; they were left in their former squalor and ignorance while even greater sacrifices were demanded of them: in the building of the empire; in the numerous and exhausting wars and the heavy taxation which these wars demanded; in the various public works, like the construction of Petersburg, the new capital erected in the Neva swamps. Peter's Western ways shocked the masses. They were unable to assimilate the new civilization, and they resented it. For many centuries they had been taught to regard all Western influences as heretical. Peter openly defied and humiliated the church. Unlike his father, Tsar Alexis, he had no piety and no reverence. He still worshipped at the church's shrines because he was used to them and had no thought of changing them. He was even devout on occasion and would sometimes sing in the church choir. But he continually reminded the ecclesiastical hierarchy of its subservient role.

Peter is to some extent a precursor of the Bolshevist godless. Not that he wanted to destroy religion, but he had strange moods and whims. A tireless statesman and soldier, he nevertheless had occasional lapses into wild orgies and drinking bouts, during the course of which he would organize mock pageants which he called "All-Buffoon Councils," with clowns and drunken courtiers impersonating priests and bishops, presided over by an "All-Buffoon Pope."

To Peter's revolution from above, the people reacted by a revolution from below. The Raskol flared up once more. Weird sects and extreme social and mystical teachings stirred the masses. The tsar was denounced as the Antichrist, and once more the rumor spread that the end of the world was near. Peter dealt ruthlessly with the Raskolniki and other rebel sects. They were tortured and executed, imprisoned, or banished. He saw in them an element of blind reaction, of frenzied opposition to the new ways which were to bring light to Russia and turn her into a world power. He was intent on one object, and those who imposed obstacles to its attainment were crushed. Even his son and heir, Alexis, he did not spare. When the young man joined the opposition, he had him arrested and tortured, finally slaying him with his own hands.

The masses surrendered. But they withdrew into themselves, more isolated and forlorn than they had ever been, jealously preserving the faith which the "enlightened" court despised. Thus the gulf yawned between the people and the upper classes. Socially and economically, it was gradually bridged when Peter's successors applied themselves to improving the people's condition. But spiritually it remained. This is one of the tragic elements of Russia's modern history. The soul of Russia has been cleft in two.

Nevertheless, this very tragedy was to be a creative factor. Russia's great thinkers, writers, poets, and social and religious leaders worked under the stimulus of pain to heal the breach between the upper classes and the people. They were aware that in their people obscure, but extraordinarily creative, forces were latent. And the spiritually cultured *élite* eagerly listened for the voice of their people and sought to render it articulate in literature, art, and ethics. This ardent desire to rediscover the secret soul of the common people was the source of the movement known as Russian populism.

But Peter himself, though he ruthlessly broke down the ancient mould of the Muscovite tsardom, was not a phenomenon foreign to the national genius. He is profoundly Russian in that he chose the extreme path and wandered on the brink of the precipice. He mocked the church and stripped it of its magnificent trappings, but there was something religious in the very zeal with which he served Russia. Though he acted as an almighty ruler, he was not an arbitrary tyrant. It has been pointed out that as the Russian emperor he was an autocrat very much like the other European autocrats of his time; yet he did not go so far as Louis XIV of France, who declared that he *was* the state. Peter was not intoxicated with his own power. What he served was not himself but his country. He destroyed the past because, like Krijanitch, he firmly believed in the future. He saw the great empire emerging from its century-old seclusion, gaining access to the sea (the window on Europe), which alone could grant it breathing space, and opening its gates to the creative forces of the West. Peter expresses one of Russia's deepest aspirations—the desire for universality, for brotherhood with the whole world. His peculiar radicalism is the manifestation of the spirit which historical circumstances—the break with Rome, the Mongol domination, and the constant threat of foreign invasion—had stifled for many centuries. Actually, Russia's prolonged isolation and seclusion had been an anomaly.

"The Russian mission," writes Dostoievsky, "is undisputably European and universal. To become a real Russian, to become entirely Russian, perhaps only means to become the brother of all men, an *all-man* . . . Among all the peoples, the Rus-

sian heart is most inclined to an all-human, brotherly union
. . . The people of Europe do not know how dear they are to
us!" [1]

Thus, in his violent extremes and his passionate desire to
hasten Russia's growth, Peter reflected this confused necessity
of fulfilling a world mission. Though he broke and lacerated
Russia's body and disrupted her soul, he liberated her from
inertia and complacence. Russia first resisted, then understood
him. She yielded to his impulse, unfolded and developed the
latent forces which were to bring her closer and closer to
Western Europe. The magic plant grew and blossomed. A
hundred and fifty years after Peter's death, the Russian genius
bore its fruit in great literature and great humanistic philosophy. Through Tolstoy and Dostoievsky, Russia gave her message to the world. But the first Russian to incarnate this
spirit of universality was the poet Alexander Pushkin. In the
words of the Russian journalist A. Herzen, "The people re-
sponded to Peter's reforms by giving birth to Pushkin."

If we were to confine ourselves to the consideration of
Russia's purely religious and typically Orthodox thought patterns, there would be no place for Pushkin in this book. This
poet, who may be said to have created the modern Russian
language and whose work was a fount of inspiration for
modern Russian literature, was animated by none of his
people's characteristic piety. Though he submitted to the
outward observances of Orthodoxy, as all Russian noblemen
were expected to do, he did not absorb its spirit. Berdiaev
calls him a man of the Renaissance. He was neither poor in
spirit like St. Sergius and St. Theodosius nor tormented and
fanatical like Avvakum. In his youth, he wrote anti-religious
verse, which was the cause of his prolonged exile.

Pushkin was of African descent, his mother having been
the granddaughter of an Abyssinian prince who served at

[1] Speech on Pushkin's Anniversary, June 8, 1880. See Dostoievsky,
Complete Works.

Peter's court, and the hot Mediterranean blood spoke more loudly than Slavic mysticism. And yet, Pushkin's spiritual experience corresponds so closely with that of the Russian people as a whole, he is, like Peter, such a peculiarly national phenomenon, that the entire Russian culture of the two past centuries has felt the impress of his genius. His poems and short stories, his historical essays and plays, are perfect works of art. His literary style has scarcely been surpassed. When we speak modern Russian, we speak Pushkin's tongue, for he actually recreated and remodeled the language of his time.

Pushkin was gay, lighthearted, and dissipated, but his destiny, the story of his life and death, is marked with a mysterious beauty and sadness. This undisciplined young man who was a joyful companion at officers' drinking parties and a frivolous lover, was exalted and profoundly serious in his creative moods. He wrote the most bitter epigrams of his time and the noblest epic poems. He is the author of erotic verse which no publisher has dared to print, and he has written the gentlest of love songs, which inspired Tchaikovsky. He was closely linked to the first Russian revolutionary movement, the conspiracy of the "Decembrists," whose leaders were his intimate friends. And he was at the same time the poet of Peter the Great and of the Russian Empire. And like Peter the Great he had eagerly absorbed Western culture. He was a Westerner by education, whose first poems were written in French and who was influenced by the works of Byron. Pushkin never went abroad. As he wrote in one of his poems, he pined all his life for a glimpse of the Adriatic waves and the blue sky of Africa. Because of his subversive ideas, he was held suspect by the authorities and never allowed to cross the border. He was a Petersburg dandy and a typical Russian country gentleman, and as a poet he ranks with Goethe, Shakespeare, Shelley, and Musset.

In spite of his poetic genius, Pushkin would not have left such a deep impress on posterity had it not been for a circumstance which can be termed providential: at the beginning of his literary career he was banished from the capital for irreverent verse. There followed several years of enforced residence in Bessarabia and a voyage to the Caucasus. He thus acquired a wide knowledge of his own country and a deep insight into its peculiar problems. But most important to his productiveness was the fact that he was subsequently allowed to settle down in his country estate, Mikhailovskoie, in the province of Pskov, where he lived in complete retirement, in close contact with nature and with the peasantry. Pushkin was not, like Tolstoy, an advocate of the simple life, nor was he a populist in the usual sense of the word. He had no interest in social teachings. But he absorbed, almost instinctively, the creative forces of the people. He drank them in like a plant receiving its natural nourishment from the soil. From the people, and especially from his old nurse, Arina Rodionovna, Pushkin learned the secrets of the native soul and the dialect of the native tongue. He abandoned the pompous, artificial style used by the poets of his time and plunged into the language of Russian folklore, thus bringing about a revolution in Russian literature.

We have previously said that we Russians all speak like Pushkin. It would be more correct to say that we all speak like Pushkin's nurse, Arina Rodionovna. The poet dedicated much of his verse to the beautiful and brilliant Petersburg ladies, but one of the most famous of his poems is dedicated to Arina Rodionovna. Full of tender gratitude, Pushkin calls her "the companion of my austere days." Indeed, these years spent at Mikhailovskoie were years of disciplined work and meditation. The frivolous, temperamental, Petersburg dandy had become conscious of the poet's unique vocation: "You are a king: live alone," he wrote.

In another of his poems, *The Prophet*, he painted an even more exalted picture of the poet's mission: he speaks of an angel who appeared to him in the desert as to the biblical prophet, tearing out his tongue and replacing it by a serpent's sting, putting in his breast a burning charcoal, filling his ears with a great noise:

> And the voice of God called to me:
> Rise, prophet, see and hear,
> Be filled by my will,
> And crossing seas and lands
> Burn the hearts of men with thy words.

Pushkin had written irreverent verse in his youth; he was not a devout son of the church. But in *The Prophet* he revealed a religious soul; he attained a vision of God, of the universe, and of his own vocation as a poet, which reveals the deeply spiritual sources of his genius. He had a mysterious cosmic sense which allowed him to see and hear things hidden from the ordinary man.

At Mikhailovskoie Pushkin wrote *Eugene Onegin*, a novel in verse describing the life of Petersburg society and the more homely scenes of the Russian countryside. "*Eugene Onegin*," writes the critic D. Mirsky, "is full of that peculiarly Russian realism which is poetical without idealizing and without surrendering anything of reality. It is the realism of Lermontov's and Turgenev's novels, of the best of Tchekhov and of Tolstoy's *War and Peace*. *Eugene Onegin* can therefore be considered the fountainhead of the Russian novel." [2]

It is also in *Eugene Onegin* that we find for the first time a portrait of the Russian woman with her fundamental traits: her simplicity, her loyalty, her constancy and courage, her infinite capacity for love and sacrifice. Tatiana, the heroine of the poem, is the prototype of the feminine characters described by later Russian novelists. And after more than a hundred years, Tatiana is as popular in Russia as she was when Pushkin first conjured her up.

After many years of solitude and exile Pushkin obtained his pardon and the permission to live in Petersburg. But this was

[2] Mirsky, *op. cit.,* p. 115.

only an apparent liberation. Actually, he was still suspected of subversive tendencies, and the publication of his work was placed under strict control. True, he was dispensed from the usual formalities of censorship; but he was subjected to even more rigorous restrictions in that Tsar Nicholas I, aided by the Police General, Count Benckendorff, was his personal censor.

Pushkin had begun his literary career under the reign of the liberal-minded and mystical Tsar Alexander I. Alexander's brother, Nicholas, who succeeded him, was the stern and inflexible ruler who had crushed the Decembrist revolution and instituted an iron régime which had two instruments, the bureaucracy and the police. The last period of Pushkin's brief life was spent in this oppressive atmosphere, and more than once he looked back with nostalgia on the years of his enforced retirement at Mikhailovskoie.

In Petersburg the poet passed through the tragic spiritual ordeal which culminated in his death. Soon after his return to the capital, Pushkin married the beautiful, but cold and heartless, Nathalie Gontcharova, a young woman who entirely failed to understand her husband's genius. Her indifference deeply wounded him, and though she was a faithful wife and bore him several children, her worldliness and the admiration which her beauty aroused even in the tsar filled the poet with sombre jealousy. Pushkin was trapped. His wife's love of brilliant society and the court interfered with his work, which was already hampered by His Majesty's censorship. The Pushkins were poor. To satisfy Nathalie's whims, the poet was now obliged to seek means of increasing his resources. He contracted debts. Known all his life for his independence, he now curried favor with the tsar. He applied for an official's post and was attached to the archives of the Ministry of Foreign Affairs, whereupon he gave up creative work almost entirely and devoted himself to historical research.

At home he found no peace. His wife was courted by a young officer of the guards, of French origin. George Dantes was tall, handsome, and fair-skinned. Pushkin was swarthy, shaggy, thick-lipped. The African strain was strong in him. When he took his wife to dances, their friends compared them to Pluto and Venus. Everyone talked about Nathalie's affair with Dantes, although actually it did not go beyond an imprudent flirtation.

One day Pushkin received an anonymous letter of a particularly insulting character. It was written in the form of a diploma conferring upon the poet the title of outraged husband. Pushkin's African passions flared. He provoked George Dantes to a duel, rejecting all offers of reconciliation. On a grim, frozen, winter afternoon Pushkin was mortally wounded by his rival in a snow-covered park on the outskirts of Petersburg. He was brought home in a state of acute suffering, but fully conscious and aware that his end was near. His wife manifested so little grief that he called her to his bedside and advised her to show more concern, lest people should think ill of her. He neither rebuked her nor spoke of Dantes. Hearing of the fatal encounter, Tsar Nicholas sent his aide-de-camp to the dying poet to inform him that His Majesty "deigned to forgive him." Pushkin became delirious. Just as he was drifting into unconsciousness, he pointed to his books, saying: "These are my friends." Soon after, he breathed his last. He was thirty-eight years old.

After Pushkin's death there were only a few rubles left, scarcely enough to pay his debts, and Nathalie, as the widow of Russia's greatest poet, was pensioned by the state. But the tsar, knowing Pushkin's popularity among subversive elements and fearing a public demonstration, ordered that the poet should be buried at night, outside of Petersburg. A detachment of armed police accompanied his body to its last resting place, and Nathalie was requested to stay at home.

Although the record of the circumstances surrounding Pushkin's death reads like the climax of some great play, exalted and yet profoundly human, there was no emotionalism about Pushkin himself. He loved and hated, wrote his immortal poems and fought duels (he had quite a number of them before his fatal encounter with Dantes) with the simplicity and manliness which are the attributes of the great. His conflict with the tsar and his unhappy marriage darkened his life with tragedy. Yet in his creative moods he is as clear and harmonious as a cloudless summer day.

Much has been written about Pushkin, beginning with the essays of his contemporary the brilliant critic Bielinsky and ending with the learned works of Soviet commentators. It is almost impossible to sum up all that has been said of him. He is the poet of the early revolutionary movement: his subversive poems, which provided incitement to rebellion and even to regicide, filled the tsarist police with consternation. And he is the poet of Russia's might. In *Poltava* and *The Bronze Horseman* he has painted immortal portraits of Peter the Great. In his play *Boris Godunov* he has depicted ancient Moscow with a profound sense of national history. He is the greatest of Russian lyrical poets, and no other Russian writer has equalled the mastery of his prose. His style has the discipline of classicism blended with the colour and fertility of Russian folklore. Although his depiction of tsars and princes and the sophisticated dandies of Petersburg society is clear and true, he had a direct, instinctive knowledge of the psychology of the common people, of nature, of the primitive soil in which Russian culture is rooted.

All this has been written a thousand times about the miracle of Pushkin. But doubtless the most discerning words ever spoken of him were uttered by Dostoievsky in his "Author's Diary" and in his famous speech on the poet's fiftieth anniversary. Dostoievsky said that Pushkin "was not only a Russian, but the first wholly Russian man because he was the first to voice his people's genius."

He bowed down before the truth of the people and acknowl-
edged it as his own truth. In spite of all the people's faults, he
realized the great significance of its spirit and took this truth into
his heart. . . . Pushkin was the first to understand that the Russian is no slave, in spite of century-old slavery. . . . He loved the
people, not only because of its suffering. Suffering inspires pity,
and pity is so often linked with disdain. Pushkin loved all that the
people loved, venerated all that it respected. He loved Russian
landscapes passionately, he loved the Russian country-side. He
was not the charitable, humanitarian master pitying the peasants
and their sad lot—he was a man whose heart itself was the incarnation of the simple folk. . . . Pushkin's word is till today a new
word, and not only a new word, but an unknown and as yet an
undeciphered word.[3]

What was this unknown word uttered by the author of
Eugene Onegin? Dostoievsky tells us that it was the call to
universality: "Had Pushkin lived longer," he exclaims, "there
would be less misunderstanding among us than now exists!
But God decided differently, and he took his great secret to his
grave. And now, we are trying to guess this secret without
him." [4]

Pushkin wrote that his name would live for ever in the
memory of the Russian people. His prediction has been fulfilled, and even the Revolution, which has destroyed so many
Russian cultural values, has not dispelled this memory. Indeed,
he still remains Russia's greatest national poet: he forms an
indissoluble bond between the past and the present. On the
hundredth anniversary of Pushkin's death, fifty years after
Dostoievsky's speech, hundreds of essays, illustrated albums,
biographical sketches, and scholarly works devoted to the poet
appeared in Soviet Russia. His works were translated into the
tongues of all the nationalities forming the Soviet Union. This,
too, he had predicted when he wrote that he would be remem-

[3] Dostoievsky, *Pushkin, Lermontov i Nekrassov*. See "Author's Diary"
in *Complete Works*.
[4] Dostoievsky, *loc. cit.*

bered and honored from the Finnish coast to sunny Crimea.

Statistics of Soviet public libraries and book clubs indicate that *Eugene Onegin* is one of the most widely circulated and popular books in Russia. Tatiana remains the beloved heroine of Russian youth, although this melancholy and poetic figure of romantic Russia little resembles the dynamic and emancipated girl of the Soviet. A story related in the Moscow press bears witness to the poet's survival. One day a group of boys belonging to the communist youth movement were led by their instructors to Pushkin's monument. The boys looked up at the curly-headed, thick-lipped man gazing down on them from his bronze pedestal. For a moment they stood in silence, wondering what to say. Then one of them stepped up, smiled, extended his hand, and joyfully exclaimed: "Good morning, Pushkin!"

VIII

The White Flame

NINETEENTH CENTURY RUSSIA was quickened by a literary and cultural renaissance, but for the Russian hierarchy it was a period of decline. Peter the Great had dealt a heavy blow to religious life when he secularized his empire.

It may seem strange that a country which had appeared to present an almost flawless theocracy should have yielded so readily to secular influences. But the deep transformation was not entirely the work of Peter. When he ascended the throne he found a church already weakened by the Raskol. Ecclesiastical authority had been profoundly shaken by Nikon's violences. In fact the Russian people had revolted against the patriarchate long before it was suppressed by their sovereign. The secularization of the Third Rome had one immediate effect. By restricting the authority of the church hierarchy, it released that tremendous spiritual potential which had already drifted loose from its moorings. Free of the church's sanctions, these forces now developed unchecked.

During the centuries which followed Peter's reforms, Russia's spiritual dynamism revealed itself most powerfully. But it assumed new, and often anarchical, forms, as may be observed in the various sects which flourished during that period. Sometimes it was clothed in a misty idealism of Western hue : Freemasonry, Illuminism, Protestantism, and romantic Catholicism all found devotees in Petersburg's high society.

These released energies fed yet another stream, the powerful stream of protest—ideological, sociological, and political— which now began to swell. Of this stream of protest we shall make further analysis. It becomes, indeed, the central theme of

Russian literature and of Russian political thought. As Nicholas Berdiaiev has often pointed out, the Russian revolutionary movement, even in its most extreme forms, still retains a religious impulse.

The Russian sects have been the object of special research and form a separate chapter of the history of the Russian church. Some of them were formed as the result of the infiltration of Protestant and rationalist influences; the Baptists, the Mennonites, the Dukhobors, and the Evangelists attracted a number of followers, and their converts sharply broke away from the main stem of Orthodoxy. Their teachings are characterized by a deep attachment to the Gospels, evangelical simplicity, and a strong ethical undercurrent. The members of these sects have constantly been in opposition to the state, not on political but on moral grounds. Many of them are conscientious objectors who reject government authority and all legal institutions, in this way manifesting the feeling of the Russian people that authority based on force is unrighteous. Tolstoy's doctrines give literary expression to this theme, but it is as old as Russia herself.

Nevertheless, Protestantism as such has not been deeply rooted in the Russian soul. At least it did not stir, it seems, her elemental emotions. As we have seen, Russia did not pass through the spiritual crisis of the Reformation. The Russian sectary may profess rationalistic doctrines, but he is not a rationalist but a visionary. He resembles not so much the Puritan of the West as the three holy men in Tolstoy's famous short story who, although they had forgotten the prayers of the official church, were nevertheless typical Russian Startzy.

There were groups outside the church other than the Protestant sects. The Raskol still flourished, even in its priestless forms. For the most part, the Raskolniki led the arduous life in their agricultural communities, jealously guarding the ikons painted by the masters of pre-Nikon days and constantly awaiting the day of judgment. They were known as men of austere life, pious, sober, industrious, and honest in their dealings with others. The use of tobacco, which they called the devil's herb, was strictly prohibited in their communities. Some of their number abandoned the arduous life and became prosperous tradesmen. A good proportion of the Moscow merchants who attained considerable wealth and power belonged to the old Raskolnik families.

And there were other streams whose waters were far more troubled and obscure: weird, morbid sects such as the *Chlysty,* who formed secret communities which they called "Ships" and who elected male and female leaders known as "Christs" and "Virgins." One of their branches the *Skoptzy* ("Castrates"), practised self-mutilation.

Both Chlysty and Skoptzy considered sin (insofar as it led to repentance) a means of sanctification. Therefore they permitted and even encouraged immorality. During the meetings of the Ships they danced and whirled in order to attain a religious ecstasy which subsequently degenerated into the most repulsive and morbid forms of eroticism. It is probable that Rasputin belonged to a Chlysty sect; his obscure teaching, his sensuality, and his famous orgies are characteristic. Although their teachings spread among the masses especially, the Chlysty and Skoptzy numbered members of Petersburg society among their adherents. Their activities were eventually checked and the practice of self-mutilation severely punished. It cannot be said that this degeneracy is in any way characteristic of the authentic religious spirit of the Russian people.

The Protestant sects and the Raskolniki still form important groups of the Russian population. On the eve of the Revolution the number of their adherents was estimated at about twelve million. Under the Bolsheviki, they were at first encouraged, for the godless considered them an element in opposition to the official church. Later, however, their importance from this point of view became minimized, and the dissidents suffered as great persecution as did the Orthodox. Because of their courage, their high moral standards, and their fidelity to their own beliefs, they are highly respected, but the majority of the Russian population has rallied around the Orthodox Church. Russian history clearly indicates that at times of national emergency it is the official church as an organized body which unites and inspires the masses. There is, as we have observed, a continuity in Russian religious life.

This continuity explains the stubborn resistance offered by the Russian people to communist anti-religious propaganda. The popular attachment to the faith has often puzzled foreign observers and even awakened their scepticism. How is it possible, they ask, that a church which had been so disorganized and weak before the Revolution that it seemed about to crumble under the first assault, has found such strong support as to have survived the onslaught?

Actually, it was the *state organization* of the church which was weak. The Russian ecclesiastical bureaucracy did crumble under the first assault, but the spiritual vitality of the church was not dependent on this administrative machine. It had its own shrines, its own secluded world where glowed what Berdiaev calls "the white flame of Orthodoxy." The luminance of this flame appeared in the person of that great spiritual teacher of the early nineteenth century, Saint Seraphim of Sarov, and in a remarkable community, the Optyna Pustyn, which was to exercise a profound influence on Russian religious thought.

St. Seraphim is Russia's most popular saint. His popularity is parallel to that of Little St. Theresa in the West: his image can be found in every Russian home. The ikons of Seraphim usually represent him praying in his cell or meditating in the woods while the bear which he has tamed watches him. He is seen as a little old man with long white hair and a white beard, and there is, in the almost childlike naiveté of his expression, something which makes one think of the Curé d'Ars. It is difficult to imagine a personal resemblance between the Staretz, lost in the depths of the Russian woods, and the priest of the peaceful French country parish. Nevertheless this comparison has been stressed by the Russians themselves. There are those who believe that the Curé d'Ars had somehow been informed of the life and teaching of St. Seraphim. Indeed there is a certain affinity between their mystical paths. But this may be an instance of what has frequently been held a fact —that great ascetics meet on the heights of contemplation.

Seraphim, whose name in the world was Prokhor Moshnin, was born in Kursk in 1759, the son of a devout merchant. When he was nineteeen years old, he entered the Sarov Monastery. After his ordination, he received daily communion for a year (a practice which was not usual in Russia), but soon, like the Seekers of Silence, he heard the call of the woods. He retired to a hut which he himself built five miles from the monastery. Here he spent thirty-one years in solitude.

For a thousand nights he prayed, standing on a stone. He never left the wood, and he received no visitors, for he had bound himself to absolute silence. He lived on a few vegetables from his own little plot, and sometimes he would go entirely without food. He faced innumerable hardships and dangers living among the wild beasts of the forest; and on one occasion he was attacked by a brigand. Like the Curé d'Ars, he was tempted and persecuted by the devil. But he tamed the beasts and repulsed the evil spirits. After thirty-one years, he opened his cell to the people and began to teach what he called *the way to the acquisition of the Holy Ghost*.

Motovilov, a merchant of the neighborhood who was Seraphim's disciple, wrote an account of the saint's life and teaching which is the main biographical source concerning him. Seraphim healed the sick by prayer and comforted the suffering. His spiritual advice was sought by men of wealth and influence and by the simple folk. Great sinners repented and led a life of mortification under his guidance. He was gentle and compassionate, yet he would sometimes treat his spiritual children with extreme severity. According to the tradition of the Startzy, he demanded from them complete obedience to his direction. Once he ordered a woman who came to him to prepare herself for death, saying that she was to give up her life in order to save another soul. The woman obeyed the Staretz and made all the necessary preparations. In a few days she was taken ill and died, just as Seraphim had told her she would.

This is a striking example of the absolute and sometimes awe-inspiring authority exercised by the Staretz. Yet there was nothing sombre about him. His biographer Professor Il'in describes him as enveloped in a "dazzling seraphic whiteness." Motovilov relates that on a certain winter night he accompanied Seraphim into the thick of the woods. The disciple asked the hermit to reveal to him something of the truth he had attained through contemplation.

"Look at me," Seraphim commanded.

Motovilov lifted his eyes and was almost blinded by the light that shone from the old man's face. It was "as if a thousand sparks fell from his eyes, setting the woods ablaze." Seraphim, thus transfigured, appeared "more dazzling than the middle of the sun." And although they stood in deep snow; Motovilov felt a warm glow, and a great joy filled his heart.[1]

Seraphim taught his spiritual children to acquire the Holy Ghost through simplicity, a continual living in the divine presence, and a dedication of all thoughts and deeds to God. "Good deeds," he said, "are candles lit before our Lord." He had many visions, and his brethren more than once beheld him in a state of levitation. One day as he was singing the Mass, they saw the Blessed Virgin bending over him and heard her words, "This is one of our kin."

Like the Curé d'Ars and St. Theresa of Lisieux, Seraphim is a comparatively recent saint; he is a familiar figure, closer to us than the older Russian mystics. His way to the acquisition of the Holy Ghost is both active and contemplative. Although it

[1] Il'in, *Sviatoi Serafim*.

took him thirty years to accumulate his wisdom, he placed it within easy reach of every layman. Like St. Theresa of Lisieux, he taught the "little way." During his life his mystic path was communicated to few, but after his death his influence began to spread. The "dazzling candle of seraphic whiteness" was rediscovered in Russia on the eve of the Revolution.

Another center of spiritual life was the Optyna monastery in the midst of the thick forests of the Kaluga region. This sanctuary, whose white walls and pale-blue cupolas were described by Dostoievsky in *The Brothers Karamazov*, has been immortalized in Russian literature.

Founded in the Middle Ages by the brigand Opta, who had repented towards the end of his turbulent life and spent many years in prayer and mortification, Optyna was rebuilt and became a large community in the early thirties of the nineteenth century. The first Startzy to extend its influence were the priests Leonidas and Makarius. They followed the teachings of Paissy Vilitchkovsky, an Ukrainian monk who exercised a deep influence on Russian monastic life. Paissy was himself a Staretz who had spent the early part of his life at Mount Athos. When he later became the member of a Moldavian community, he revived and fostered the great patristic tradition. He wrote a number of learned works in Greek, which the Optyna monks translated and printed. Thus the Greek tradition was restored to Russia after a long hiatus caused by distrust and hostility, and this stimulus quickened intellectual activity not only in the monasteries but also in the divine academies.

However, the Optyna Startzy did not allow Greek ascetic teachings to obscure the essentially Russian pattern of moderation and spiritual soberness. They were austere but not over-rigorous, and thus they were able to draw to their monasteries men of the world whom extreme ascetic practices would have kept away. Like all Startzy, they demanded obedience to spiritual direction, but they did not prescribe the impossible. From all parts of Russia visitors came to relax in the silence of the forest and be instructed by the monks. Among these visitors there were writers and leaders of cultural circles. Gogol, who came to Optyna several times, described it with enthusiasm:

I have never seen anyone like these monks. It seemed that each of them conversed with the celestial . . . even the lay brothers impressed me by their angelic mildness, the luminous simplicity of their ways. . . . Already as we approach the monastery, a few miles away from it, we feel the fragrance. Everything becomes more friendly, the people bow lower, sympathy towards man deepens.

Indeed the middle way of the Startzy, their deep spirituality mingled with gentleness and love, seemed to have exerted its influence on everyone in the vicinity of the monastery, on even the peasants tilling the soil. It pervaded nature itself, turning the sombre woods into an abode of peace and ineffable joy.

It was at Optyna that the turbulent and tormented Constantine Leontiev, one of the most brilliant minds of his time, took refuge. This writer, who had held the office of Russian Consul at Constantinople, Berdiaev calls "a solitary thinker." He was a ruthless critic of modern Western civilization, which to his mind was corrupt and falling into disintegration. After experiencing an acute spiritual crisis he became a fervent adherent of the Orthodox Church, but he wanted Russia to return to Byzantine sources, which he believed to be the fountainhead of true spirituality and true culture. Before coming to Optyna he had made a solemn vow to become a monk, but the Startzy advised him to remain in the world and pursue his literary work for the time being. He settled down at Optyna in a small building which has ever since been called "the Consul's house." Here he devoted himself to writing. One may say that most of his religious inspiration was derived from the instruction which he received from the Startzy. Towards the end of his life, true to his vow, he made his religious profession.

It was at Optyna that Gogol discovered the vivifying sources of faith which were to transform his life. He, too, had gone through a spiritual crisis and had been tormented by doubts and temptations until he found his way to the forest *thebaide*. Had it not been for Optyna, he would probably never have written his *Divine Liturgy*, one of the most profound and beautiful of his works.

Ivan Kireievsky, the founder of the Slavophile movement, corresponded with the Optyna monks and often visited the monastery. Soloviev and Dostoievsky went there in 1878, and Tolstoy, the eternal searcher, was another visitor. Even when he was estranged from the church, he remembered the spirit of Optyna. In his flight from his home in 1910, which culminated in his death in a railway station, he took shelter for a time at Shamardino, a women's convent which had been founded by the Optyna Startzy and which followed their teachings.

Thus it can be said that the spiritual sources of Russia's modern literature welled up in this forest *thebaide* whose monks were scholars as well as profoundly spiritual men. Here we behold the most exalted aspect of Russian Startchestwo. The union of culture and spirituality finds its fullest expression in the personality of Father Ambrose, the successor of Leonidas and Makarius, whom Dostoievsky knew and whose immortal picture he painted in *The Brothers Karamazov*, for Staretz Zossima, the spiritual teacher of Aliesha Karamazov, is none other than this Optyna monk: [1]

[1] This fact has been contested by some critics. Constantine Leontiev, for instance, states that Dostoievsky gave a distorted image of the Staretz. Nevertheless it is certain that even though Dostoievsky may have presented his own interpretation of the teaching and personality of Ambrose, his character Zossima gives true expression to the spirit of the Startchestwo.

ALEXANDER PUSHKIN

It was said that so many people had for years past come to confess
their sins to Father Zossima and to entreat him for words of
advice and healing, that he had acquired the keenest intuition
and could tell from an unknown face what a newcomer wanted,
and what was the suffering on his conscience. He sometimes
astounded and almost alarmed his visitors by his knowledge of
their secrets before they had spoken a word.[2]

Thus Dostoievsky wrote of Zossima, thinking of Ambrose who
had perhaps astounded and alarmed him when he visited the
monk's cell. The entire atmosphere of *The Brothers Karamazov* is pervaded with the light of the mystic flame which
burned at Optyna.

A supernatural fragrance seems to emanate from the darkest
pages of this novel. Zossima receiving callers in his cell, com-
forting the sick and the unfortunate, teaching Aliesha the way
of saintliness—all this becomes a living reality. And as the
younger Karamazov kneels down to kiss the earth in an
ecstasy of love and joy, we can hear the rustle of the Optyna
trees and see the peaceful fields blessed by the angelic men.

[2] Dostoievsky, *The Brothers Karamazov*, p. 27.

IX

Blood on Ice

IN HIS POEM *The Bronze Horseman* Pushkin describes the adventures of a young madman who defies the bronze statue of Peter the Great in a Petersburg square. Poor Eugene's malady follows upon the loss of his betrothed, who perishes in the flood which sweeps over Petersburg when the Neva overflows its banks during the spring thaw. He roams through the streets in despair until he comes to Peter's monument.[1] The bronze Peter, crowned with laurel, his hand extended in an imperious gesture, is mounted on a steed which seems about to gallop into the air.

Eugene accuses the bronze horseman of being the author of his personal tragedy, for it was Peter who built the new capital on the banks of the Neva, thus exposing the poor people to the terrible floods which periodically devastated the area. As he lashes out his bitter invective against the tsar, the bronze horse with its imperious rider leaps from its pedestal and gallops through the streets, pursuing the madman until it finally tramples him under its furious hoofs.

Pushkin wrote his poem during the later period of his life, after he had experienced both Nicholas's oppression and his favor. It is a strange, eery poem, and its descriptions of the great tsar and of Petersburg are unforgettable. It gives us the feeling of the crushing force of the Russian Empire and of the impassioned protest of the individual against this force which threatened him with annihilation. The great struggle which

[1] This famous statue still stands in the square because the Bolshevists have respected the memory of Russia's empire builder.

was to take place between the tsar and his people was witnessed in its beginnings by Pushkin himself. In fact it was in Pushkin's youth, during the reign of Alexander I, that the first seeds of rebellion were sown.

The early part of Alexander's reign was a period of national unity. Napoleon's invasion of Russia had awakened ardent patriotism. As in the days of Dmitry Donskoy and in the troubled times, all Russia had rallied against the invader. After Napoleon's defeat, Alexander's prestige both in Russia and abroad was immense; his personal charm, intelligence, and culture made him a romantic figure. His admirers called him "our angel," and his court, during these early years of his reign, was enveloped in a quasi-mystical atmosphere.

The influence of the eighteenth century free thinkers still prevailed among the members of the older generation, but the new cultural élite was no longer satisfied with Voltaire. Nor did it find sufficient spiritual food in the official church. The Optyna Startzy had not yet extended their influence, and St. Seraphim did not create a unifying center as had St. Sergius of Radonezh; the enlightened Petersburg gentry was scarcely aware of him. Pushkin, who was his contemporary, had probably never heard of him. Petersburg society turned Westward in search of fresh religious inspiration.

The influence of mystical Freemasonry strongly tinged with Rosicrucian teaching was making itself felt at that time. Emperor Alexander himself was interested in the movement. He also supported the Bible society brought to Russia by an English cleric. He was for a time impressed by the mystical utterances and prophecies of Baroness Krudener,[2] and there

---

[2] Baroness Varvara Julia Krudener, née Fitinhof, was a Russian by birth and a preacher influenced by the German nineteenth century mystics of Protestant hue and by the biblical society. The Tsar met her shortly after the Congress of Vienna and was deeply impressed by her "prophecies." He was said to have consulted her on several occasions and it was rumoured that she inspired him with the idea of the Holy Alliance. Her influence, however, was very much exaggerated, and Alexander soon tired of the "prophetess."

was a period when he was attracted by Catholicism, as were
other members of the aristocracy. The ideas of the German
mystic school—Boehme, Yung-Stilling, and Eckarthausen—
spread through Russia. So did the writings of St. Martin, the
French Illuminist. Some of these typically Western religious
influences penetrated to the masses, mingling with native mystical currents. The Chlysty, for instance, were familiar with
Freemasonry, and the German mystics' interpretations of the
Bible were utilized by Russian Protestant sects. Practically
every kind of religious current found its way into Russia. And
they all had one element in common—that of protest against
the state church, in many instances against the state itself. The
injustices of organized power, of bureaucratic rule, and especially of serfdom were strongly felt.

Russian Freemasonry was profoundly humanitarian. The
movement had started under Empress Catherine at the end of
the eighteenth century. At that time, the Freemason Novikov
attacked serfdom and was interned in the Schlusselburg fortress for subversiveness, and another writer, Alexander Radistchev, was exiled to Siberia for causing social unrest. Although
Radistchev was not a mystic (he still belonged to the old generation of free thinkers) his exalted plea on behalf of the common man, his hatred of oppression and slavery, are of an
almost mystical character. His famous utterance "My soul is
smitten with the suffering of man" is the motto of the Russian
movement of emancipation.

When, after Napoleon's defeat, Alexander I led his armies
Westward and entered Paris, the young officers of the guard
who accompanied him beheld for the first time the new world
born of the French Revolution. From this "fabulous campaign," as it was called, young Russian noblemen brought
back new political and social ideas, new dreams of a society
founded on just principles. Alexander was not opposed to these
aspirations. He even encouraged them in his entourage. He

had been educated by the liberal Swiss scholar Laharpe, and he contemplated the creation of a constitutional régime in Russia. With the aid of his minister Speransky, he undertook the revision of the laws of the empire. He was hospitable to new ideas. When secret societies supported by the officers of the guard cropped up here and there, he closed his eyes. It has been said of him that he was the crowned leader of the Russian intelligentsia. Towards the end of his reign, however, he turned away from liberalism, falling under the influence of Archimandrite Photius, a sombre and reactionary ecclesiastic. Alexander now bestowed his favors on General Araktcheiev, a sadistic retrograde who ruled Russia with a rod of iron and founded the military colonies where men became slaves in uniform.

Revolted by Alexander's face-about, the secret societies intensified their activities. Pushkin, who, although not a member of any of their organizations, was in sympathy with them, then wrote his revolutionary poem *The Dagger*. The conspirators voiced their rebellion against the autocracy and against serfdom, and demanded drastic reforms. The spread of these radical ideas was encouraged by the members of the highest aristocracy, like the princes Trubetzkoy and Wolkhonsky. They were expressed in the most violent form by a young officer of the guard, Colonel Pestel, whom the political writer Alexander Herzen describes as the "first Russian socialist before the socialists."

Pestel, the poet Ryleiev, and the other young radical noblemen, most of whom wore the uniform of the guard, instigated the first Russian revolutionary outbreak, the "Decembrist" uprising, which took place immediately after the death of Alexander I on December 24, 1825. The armed Decembrists, acompanied by rebel soldiers, assembled on the Senate square in the heart of Petersburg. Emperor Nicholas I, Alexander's stern successor, rode out at the head of the troops which crushed the rebellion. The conspirators were arrested and tried after an inquest which Nicholas conducted in person. Pestel, Ryleiev, and two other leaders of the Decembrist movement were hanged, and the remaining rebels were exiled to Siberia. Only after fifty years of hard labor in exile were they allowed to return to Russia.

These men were the flower of Russian aristocracy, and Nicholas both hated and feared them. Ironically calling them "my friends of December," he tried to obliterate their names from the Russian people's memory. So crushing was their defeat that the poet Tiutchev wrote:

> O victims of senseless dreams!
> You hoped maybe
> That your sparse blood would suffice
> To melt the frozen pole.
> Blood smoked a while and flashed
> On the eternal ice,
> The iron winter breathed
> And nothing remained.

But the victory gained by the emperor was only apparent. In reality, the bronze horseman was powerless to destroy Eugene, the mad dreamer. The Decembrists lived on in the Russian memory. They were the *strastoterptzy*, the passion bearers, who were the first to suffer for this new cause. Their own courage and dignity and the heroism of their wives, who followed them to Siberia, awakened all the innate idealism in the Russian soul. And during their exile, they spread enlightenment in the wilderness. Actually, they were the precursors of the entire revolutionary movement, the currents of which then quickened. Thus the cataclysm of the twentieth century was prefigured in a rebellion which lasted only a few hours.

After the Decembrist uprising reaction set in and Nicholas I instituted a régime of dictatorship which seemed to stifle all creative life in Russia. However, neither the tsar's personal censorship nor the control exercised by his officials could check the dynamism of the new intelligentsia. This intelligentsia was something more than a cultured élite; it has been compared to a religious order in that it was austere, ascetic, and disinterested. Its representatives were not content to preach their doctrines: they sought to apply them. Their work, their personal aspirations, their loves and their friendships—in a word, their entire lives—bore the mark of their faith and were moulded by it.

These first fifty years of the Russian nineteenth century are so rich, not only in ideological development but also in human drama, that hundreds of works have been devoted to them under both the tsarist régime and the Soviet. The latter has made available to the public a series of previously unpublished documents, preserved in the archives, which throw new light on that remarkable period. And even these sources have not yet been fully utilized.

The aristocratic and romantic Decembrists were succeeded by a sterner generation of revolutionists, among whom was Alexander Herzen, whose doctrines were inspired by the French socialists. He was what was then called a Westerner, that is, he belonged to the number of Russian intellectuals who believed that Russia could achieve her full development only by adopting an entirely European civilization.

Herzen lived many years abroad in Paris and London. He was, so to speak, the first Russian political émigré. Gradually, his expectations with regard to the social order of the West were disappointed. Its revolutionary spirit, he considered too bourgeois. Once more he turned to Russia for light, this time to her people: in the primitive Russian peasant commune he saw a prototype of the perfect socialist order. Herzen was one of the first advocates of populism, the ideology of which was to be developed by his successors.

It is important to stress the fact that these forms of Russian socialism and populism had their origins independent of Marxist influences, even though Karl Marx was already shaping European socialist thought. The essential difference between Marxism and the early, non-Marxist forms of socialism is that the latter respected the human person. Contrary to the Marxist doctrine, which submits the individual to class interests, this earlier socialism retained an individualistic character. Herzen stressed the fact that the commune of the Russian peasant operated under the collectivist principle without suppressing the necessary freedom of the individual. In other words, it was founded on *personalism*.

This peasant commune which inspired Russian socialism had as its cornerstone the ancient Russian popular idea of social justice: property could be lawfully owned only by those who put their work into it. Actually, the soil belonged to no one. It was God's and the tsar's. It was distributed to those who tilled it with their own hands and who took legal possession of it only through work. An old Russian proverb says that "the peasant owns the land to which he has applied his plough, his scythe, and his axe."

Peasant land in Russia was collectively cultivated by the commune, or the MIR, as it was called. Periodically, the acres were divided among the families constituting the commune. In case of fire or drought, all the members shared the damages: they were also collectively responsible for the payment of taxes. This *krugovaia poruka* (common responsibility) was the social expression of the spirit of solidarity, of brotherhood, ingrained in the Russian people. The peasants of the MIR defended the poor against the rich, the weak against the strong. They considered that the *Kulak*, the wealthy peasant who exploited the more unfortunate ones, had broken with the ethic of the community. It was of this popular disapprobation of the Kulak that the Bolshevists took advantage when they used the MIR ideology to incite class struggle. They carried it to the extreme, directing violence against the ordinary well-to-do peasant under the pretext that he also was an exploiter: such a radical view had never been entertained by the peasants who formed the original communes.

The spirit of brotherhood which animated the MIR flows from profoundly Christian sources. It is essentially evangelical. So is the concept of property as God-given, as something which is made to be worked and developed for the common good, not to be exploited for the benefit of the few. The peasants considered that it was unrighteous to accumulate wealth at the expense of others who toiled and sweated without enjoying the fruits of their labors. The landlords who owned estates consisting of thousands of acres on which their serfs labored without adequate compensation were regarded as sinful by the Russian people.

Herzen held that the ideology of the MIR contained the fundamental principles of social justice, but he ignored its Christian basis. He was a sceptic and a positivist, and although his system retained the operating principles of the Russian peasant commune, he secularized it. This secularization of the social ideal was further pursued by Vissarion Bielinsky, one of the most outstanding literary critics of his time, who was the first to recognize the genius of Pushkin.

Bielinsky was a militant atheist who preached his socialist doctrine with fanaticism. He was the exponent of what modern terminology would call totalitarian collectivism. His friends referred to him as "the furious Vissarion." Bielinsky was not aware that in his system the rights and the dignity of the individual were gravely imperilled. On the contrary, he ardently defended human values.

I do not want the happiness which is bestowed on me if I am not previously reassured as to the fate of each of my brothers . . . the destiny of the subject, of the individual, the person, is more important than the destiny of the whole world. . . .

But he believed that the happiness of the individual was to be attained at any cost, through violence, and if necessary, even through bloodshed. He was indeed furious in his attacks: his letter to Gogol, whom he accused of obscurantism, is one of the most bitter pages of Russian polemic literature. All revolutionaries knew it by heart. He brought a harsh and ruthless note into the romanticism of the Decembrists. Bielinsky was not a nobleman but a commoner, the first prominent Russian author for whom writing was not an intellectual hobby but a profession and a means of subsistence. He may be considered the founder of the Russian middle class intelligentsia, which gradually supplanted the revolutionary gentry.

During most of his life, Bielinsky suffered from poverty and ill health. Like Pushkin, to whom he devoted his most brilliant critical essays, he died at the age of thirty-eight. His fanatical faith in the creation of a perfect social order, his impassioned protest against injustice, and his keen feeling for the pathos of oppressed human life have left burning traces in the hearts of his followers.

One of the most colorful figures of the Russian revolutionary movement is Michael Bakunin, the father of Russian anarchism. His biography reads like a novel full of fantastic adventures and melodramatic episodes. Bakunin was a young nobleman of gigantic stature and overwhelming vitality, a disciple of Hegel and Proudhon and a friend of Bielinsky. He studied in Germany and in France, where he took part in the revolutionary movement. With the composer Richard Wagner, he participated in the insurrection in Stuttgart, was arrested and brought in chains to Petersburg. Here he was interned in the famous fortress of St. Peter and St. Paul, where so many revolutionaries were to be imprisoned. From his cell he addressed an extraordinary "confession" to Tsar Nicholas I. Banished to Siberia, he escaped and fled to America. When he returned to Europe, he lived in England and Switzerland and undertook an epic struggle against Karl Marx. Towards the end of his life he participated in the Paris Commune. Even his most radical friends feared his tempestuous nature. One of them said that whereas he was most useful in preparing for a revolution, when the revolution actually broke out he would have to be shot.

Bakunin preached universal destruction. "The power of destruction," he wrote, "is a creative power." He believed in only one force, the elemental surge of the masses. If they were freed from the shackles of the state and were left to themselves, they would create the perfect social order. The true leaders of the Russian people were not the "soft" noblemen (from whose stock he himself was descended) but the brigands and rebel Cossacks like Stenka Razin and Pugatchev, who had incited the masses and led them against the tsars.

This typically Russian country gentleman became the exponent of world revolution. His thinking was deeply imbued with French socialism, with the teachings of Proudhon, with the romantic humanitarianism of the French novelist George Sand, and with the Catholic Utopianism of Lamennais. He was an atheist unaware that his social doctrine sprang from religious sources. Like Bielinsky, he believed that the extreme methods which he advocated would lead to the happiness of the individual. He hated Marx because in his eyes communism was a reactionary system, "the condemnation of the masses, forced by decrees into obedience, immobility, death." His writings denouncing the dangers of communism as creating a new form of slavery are truly prophetic. Though he was anti-religious, he was opposed to religious persecution. "If one ordered the abolition of cults, the expulsion of priests," he wrote, "you can be sure that the least religious peasants would side with the cult and the priests. . . ." [3]

One of Bakunin's friends, the Frenchman Albert Richard, wrote of him: "This great conscience who rejected conscience:

[3] Bakunin was a prolific writer and journalist. His most typical works are *Dieu et l'Etat, Lettre à Marx* and *L'Empire Knuto-Germanique,* a violent pamphlet against the German spirit of domination which in the light of present-day events is as prophetic as his attacks on Marxism. Because of his prolonged exile, most of his works were written in French

this man of faith who rejected faith: this idealist who sought to achieve his ideas by unchaining the darkest elemental forces . . . was surely one of the most curious intellectual phenomena of his time." Wagner, who gives a vivid description of Bakunin in his memoirs, called him "this monstrous man."

Strangely enough, this apostle of universal destruction was at heart a Russian patriot who looked back with admiration on Russia's empire builders. He enthusiastically praised Count Muraviev-Amursky, the famous colonizer of Siberia. He both hated and worshipped Tsar Nicholas I. Like Yury Krijanitch, he was a panslavist who recommended that the tsar unite all the Slavonic peoples under his sceptre. He wrote that "Russia could be saved only by a miracle of intelligence, of passion and of will." And he predicted that if this miracle did not occur, Russia would be plunged into the most terrible revolution.

Although Bakunin was opposed to totalitarian Marxism, he himself eventually fell under the influence of a totalitarian political leader, Netchaiev, whose personality completely dominated him. If Bakunin was, as Nicholas Berdiaiev puts it, the fantastic product of Russian aristocracy, a romantic, generous-hearted giant, Netchaiev remains the most sombre and grim character of the Russian revolutionary epic. This obscure young school master can be considered one of Lenin's precursors. In the *Catechism of a Revolutionary*, his credo, he described what he considered to be the perfect type of the political conspirator: a fanatic and an ascetic completely indifferent to ethical values, intent only on one goal: revolution. He must have "no personal interests, affairs, feelings: nothing belongs to him, not even his name." The *Catechism* stated the methods to be employed. Every sort of activity, the most cruel, most cunning, the meanest, was recommended. The conspirator might cheat, betray his closest friend, seduce the woman he loved, if the revolution required it.

Netchaiev founded a secret society "The Hatchet" which was to create a network throughout Russia. The organization of The Hatchet was maintained by iron discipline and terror-istic methods. On one occasion a member, suspected of having betrayed the society, was actually assassinated. Bakunin was horrified by these excesses in practice and turned away from his young friend. "At the end he was quite demented," he sorrowfully wrote, when Netchaiev was arrested and in-carcerated for life after a sensational trial.

Netchaiev's name is still linked with the most repulsive aspects of revolutionary amoralism, but his attitude during his imprisonment gives some indication of the unshakable integ-rity of his radicalism: he was courageous, even heroic, in fidelity to his ideal of the revolutionary ascetic and martyr: even his jailers were impressed by his stoicism.

Dostoievsky read the reports of the Netchaiev trial, and his famous novel *The Possessed* is the artist's interpretation of the Netchaiev theme. Bakunin's personality is also reflected in its pages. Dostoievsky's "Possessed" dream of a better, more equitable world, but a world based on a godless social system. They are filled with pride, believing in the power of their own reason, revolting against their Creator. And they end, like Netchaiev, by committing the most deplorable crimes. They seek to conquer pain and terror so that "there will be a new life, a new man." But they seek to attain this through the annihilation of God. *The Possessed* is a truly prophetic book inasmuch as it predicts what will happen to a society which tries to annihilate God:

Not a single nation has been founded on principles of science and reason. There never has been an example of it, except for a brief moment of folly. . . . Nations are built up by another force, which sways and dominates them, the origin of which is unknown and inexplicable. . . . It's the spirit of life, as the Scrip-tures call it, the "river of living water," the drying up of which is threatened by the Apocalypse.[4]

[4] Translated by Ivar Spector in *The Golden Age of Russian Literature,* p. 115.

Political amoralism is the dark streak in the idealism of Russian extremists. It was expressed by Netchaiev's *Catechism* and later by Lenin's ideology of militant communism. For Lenin, too, there were no transcendant ethical standards: "All that serves the Revolution is moral." Such was the slogan of the Bolshevist leaders who, like the "Possessed," sought to annihilate God in the cause of man's happiness.

This dark streak faded away after Netchaiev's trial. The frightful episode of The Hatchet filled the most radical leaders with repulsion. One may truly assert that none of them until Lenin applied the methods of the *Catechism*. But the ascetic type of social reformer, the atheist pursuing his ideal with religious fervor, prevailed in Russia. Tchernyshevsky, one of the founders of socialist populism, is a striking example of godless asceticism. So are the Nihilists Dobroliubov and Pissarev, and Mikailovsky, who has been called "the conscience-stricken nobleman." This social leader, who belonged to the Russian gentry, was deeply aware of the great wrongs committed by the upper classes against the peasants, and he demanded that these wrongs be expiated.

These are the fundamental themes of the Russian emancipation movement: populism, the ideal of social service on the part of the aristocracy as a means of expiating their wrong-doing, the establishment of a more equitable order based on the peasant commune. All these principles later developed in the movement known as "going to the people," which was conceived by the intelligentsia as an apostolate. But this movement became affected with materialistic doctrines imported from the West. It involved a rejection of the church and its teachings, a rejection not only of the official church of the Josephites but of the white flame of Radonezh and Sarov. Though the ideals of the intelligentsia were informed by the noblest humanism, revealing itself in asceticism and self-sacrifice, the search for truth and justice was godless, and as such, alien to the spirit of the people. As Berdiaev observes:

The people, that is to say chiefly the peasantry, found the point of view of the intelligentsia strange. The people still remained religious, Orthodox, and the lack of religion in the intelligentsia repelled them. The people saw a gentlefolk's pastime in the Narodniks' [Populists'] going to the people." [5]

[5] Berdiaev, *The Origin of Russian Communism,* p. 80.

X

The Catholics

As RUSSIA TURNED Westward, absorbing European culture, her contact with influences emanating from Rome was inevitably renewed. She was more open to them now than she had been during the period before Peter's reform, when Latin priests were prevented from entering Moscow. During the late eighteenth and in the early nineteenth century, the Jesuits extended their mission to Russia. They enjoyed the favor of the Empress Catherine the Great and Emperor Paul I at the time when the Society of Jesus was dissolved by the Holy See. Protection was also granted them by Alexander I when Father Surugue, a Frenchman, founded a Catholic college in Petersburg. Both Surugue and the other members of the faculty, like Father Fidèle de Grivel (also a Frenchman, who was later master of novices in a Maryland community), were active in spreading Catholicism among the Russian aristocracy. Joseph de Maistre, the famous French Catholic thinker, was at that time Sardinian ambassador to Russia. He, too, exercised considerable influence in Petersburg's high society, where he had many fervent followers. The cloud of distrust which had hung over the Latins for centuries was gradually lifted.

The Russian author Beliaiev has remarked, in describing that period, that conversion to Catholicism was considered the privilege of the aristocracy. His words are uttered half resentfully, half ironically, almost as if Catholicism were but a fleeting whim of exclusive society. Father Surugue's institution was open to young gentlemen of the Petersburg nobility. As a diplomat, Joseph de Maistre was a frequent guest at court functions and in the capital's most select circles. His brilliant intellect, profound erudition, and eloquence were most impressive, and he unquestionably contributed to the increase in the number of converts to Catholicism in Russia. His most famous convert was Madame Svetchin, the daughter of Empress Catherine's secretary and the wife of a distinguished general.

As we have seen, however, the Russian aristocracy of that time was following many Western religious trends. Not Catholicism alone, but various other European mystical and ethical teachings were being absorbed by the enlightened gentry. The masses, strongly attached to Orthodox traditions or attracted by the Raskol and the various sects, did not participate in these spiritual movements imported from the West. Yet they were in no way fleeting fancies. They corresponded to the aspiration of cultured Russians to deepen their religious life.

Conversions to Catholicism greatly disturbed Russian officials. The Orthodox were forbidden to embrace or practice another faith, under penalty of being deprived of their nationality and their property. This caused many Russian Catholic converts to go abroad. Madame Svetchin settled down in Paris, where she took part in the French religious revival of that time. She was a friend of the famous Dominican preacher Father Lacordaire, she contributed to the foundation of the Benedictine Abbey of Solesmes, and was closely associated with the Catholic political leaders Falloux and Monalembert.

"It is strange," writes Count Dmitry Tolstoy, "that a Russian is capable of playing a variety of roles everywhere, excepting Russia!" [1] Referring to Madame Svetchin as "this witty, learned and highly esteemed lady," Tolstoy, who was a staunch Orthodox, deplores the fact that she went abroad instead of devoting her energies to the service of her own country. Russian Catholics are often reproached for what their compatriots have considered desertion, but the legislation existing in Russia until

[1] See Gagarin, *Tendances catholiques dans la société Russe*.

the twentieth century made it impossible for a Catholic convert to practice his faith or have his children baptized.[2] The ban was lifted only in 1905. A Princess Galitzin, for instance, who had become a Catholic in the late sixties, journeyed to France every time she was going to give birth to a child. At that time the first trains were beginning to run in Europe. She would be driven to the border in her carriage, which would then be placed on the train and shipped to Paris bearing the expectant mother, her doctor, and her attendants.

In spite of the restrictive laws, there were many conversions; and it is quite true that they took place mostly in Petersburg's high society. Among these converts were Prince Kozlovsky, a distinguished diplomat; Countess V. N. Golovin, a prominent and extremely cultured court lady; Prince Odoyevsky; the beautiful Princess Zinaida Wolkhonsky, a cultured and artistic young woman (she introduced Italian opera to Russia) who was a friend of Pushkin and was courted by Emperor Alexander. Six members of the Galitzin family joined the Catholic Church, the most prominent of whom was Prince Demetrius, who was ordained in Baltimore and properly belongs to America's pioneer history. Several Russian noblemen entered religious orders: Balabin, Martynov, and Prince John Gagarin became Jesuits: Count Shuvalov joined the Barnabites: Wladimir Petcherin became a Redemptorist; Nathalie Narishkin was professed a sister of St. Vincent de Paul.[3]

This spread of Catholicism among distinguished Russians began to be looked upon as a serious threat to Orthodoxy. The fact that one of the Galitzins had been converted in a Jesuit college before he had attained his majority sharpened suspi-

[2] These restrictions, however, did not concern Russian citizens who were Catholics by birth, such as Poles, Lithuanians, White Russians, and Germans. Before the Revolution there were about three million Catholics in Russia in addition to those living in Poland. There were four Catholic dioceses with 1,500 churches and several seminaries.

[3] Most of the families to which these converts belonged remained Orthodox. However, there are still Catholic branches of the Galitizin and the Wolkhonsky families.

cion into open resentment. In 1815 the college was closed and
the priests were expelled from Russia. They were ordered to
leave immediately, and as the incident took place in midwinter,
Joseph de Maistre was greatly concerned in getting warm
clothing for them before they left on their long journey along
the frozen Russian roads. Soon after their departure, de
Maistre also left Russia, and subsequently Catholic influences
decreased, while the Freemasons and the Illuminist circles
gained considerable ground. At that time Alexander I was
lending his support to the Bible society which we have previously mentioned. Two Russian bishops and the Minister of
Cults officially sponsored this organization.

Nevertheless Alexander's mystical aspirations turned more
than once towards Catholicism. Was it only one of the sovereign's innumerable fancies? one of the episodes of his romantic
search of religious experience? or did he manifest more definite
intentions? Certain historians of Catholicism in Russia raise
the question whether Alexander I became a Catholic. When
the end of his life was near, the tsar is said to have entered
upon negotiations with the Holy See. The French general
Michaud, who was then at the Russian court, was dispatched
to Rome and was received by Pope Leo XII in a private
audience. It has been since rumored that important decisions
were made during that interview.[4] Alexander died during the
period when these negotiations are supposed to have been
going on.

The truth of these rumors has never been ascertained. We
are personally inclined to doubt it. Alexander may have had,
as we have pointed out, a certain interest in Catholic trends,
just as he was attracted by other forms of religious experience.
He remains one of the enigmatic figures of Russian history, and
the very circumstances of his death are shrouded in mystery.

There is a legend according to which Alexander did not die

[4] See Pierling, *L'Empereur Alexandre Ier est-il mort catholique?*; Bilbassov, *Inozemnoie Predanie ob Alexandre I.*

in 1825, in Taganrog, in the south of Russia, as was officially reported, but fled from his palace, while another man's body was placed in his casket and brought to Petersburg to be buried with the other Russian emperors. It is related that he then boarded a ship which was awaiting him and sailed for the Holy Land. Thence he is said to have returned to Russia disguised as a Staretz and to have spent the rest of his life in prayer and mortification in the city of Tomsk in Siberia, under the name of Fedor Kozmitch.

This legend is supported by the theory that Alexander had been tormented with remorse because he had participated in the assassination of his father, Emperor Paul I, or at least had tacitly approved the crime. It is conjectured that he renounced his throne in order to expiate this sin by giving the rest of his days to the service of God.

There actually was a Staretz Fedor Kozmitch who died at Tomsk in 1864. This mystery man was in some way connected with Petersburg court circles and seems to have been in touch with Emperor Nicholas I. Historians have left no stone unturned in the effort to establish his identity. Some of them have been confident that the legend of Fedor Kozmitch was pure invention; others have asserted that there was every possibility that the Staretz was none other than Alexander. In recent years the latter version has seemed to find confirmation in the fact that when the Bolshevists opened the emperors' caskets, the one supposed to contain Alexander's remains was found empty. The imperial archives in Petersburg had preserved certain documents referring to the case of Fedor Kozmitch, but the publication of these documents was prohibited, and the few scholars who had access to them were extremely guarded in their conclusions: they gave no overt credence to the legend. The Bolshevists have not made these documents known to the public.

Who was Fedor Kozmitch? Nobody has been able to answer this question satisfactorily. The house in which he had lived attracted numerous visitors after his death: pilgrims who treasured the memory of the devout Staretz, tourists, souvenir hunters, and historians eager to solve the mystery surrounding Alexander's death. They would stop before the hermit's portrait. He was shown as a tall, dignified old man with a snow-white beard, wearing the long white blouse of the Russian peasant. Whoever this mystery man was, his portrait little resembled the handsome tsar with the dreamy blue eyes and the effeminate smile whom Petersburg society had called "our angel."

The Russian Orthodox often accuse Catholic converts of having abjured not only their faith but also their nationality. By becoming Catholics, these critics contend, they cease to be Russians. To support their point of view, Russian authors usually cite as examples the converts of the early nineteenth century.

As we have seen, the Orthodox faith was closely identified with Russian culture and tradition; with the abjuration of the one, the other would inevitably undergo an alteration of what was apparently its distinct character, and there is some truth in the assertion that the members of the Russian aristocracy who embraced Catholicism at that time became, to some extent, denationalized.

Madame Svetchin, for instance, was a typical spiritual émigrée who felt more at home in Paris than in Petersburg. Prince John Gagarin, who was converted by Madame Svetchin, entered a community of French Jesuits, wrote his books in French, and never returned to Russia. As for Prince Demetrius Galitzin, he was born and educated in Holland; he never put his foot on Russian soil and can scarcely be called a Russian at all. He had no background of Russian culture or associations, and when he undertook his apostolate in America he was completely indifferent to the fact that because of his Catholic faith his country would be closed to him forever. Princess Wolkhonsky made her permanent residence in Rome, and Nathalie Narishkin belonged to the Paris community of St. Vincent de

Paul; but the most extreme case of denationalization is that of Wladimir Petcherin, a Redemptorist stationed in Ireland, who bitterly criticized Russia. He is the author of the famous poem beginning with the words:

> How sweet it is to hate one's native land
> Eagerly awaiting its destruction. . . .

If one were to confine one's observations to externals, the conclusion might easily be drawn that a Russian who has joined the Roman Church is lost to Russia. The Petersburg noblemen who joined Rome under the conditions then existing severed themselves from their native environment. They were carried away by the faith they had embraced, without looking back on those whom they left behind. But is the evidence conclusive that a process of denationalization took place interiorly?

As we follow the Russian Catholics abroad, we shall discover that they retained not merely the memory of their native land but a profound nostalgia. They constantly turned towards it in their thoughts and prayers. Except for Demetrius Galitzin, who had had practically no contact with Russia, and Madame Svetchin, who became absorbed in her Paris salon, most of them continued to display a keen interest in Russian affairs. Father John Gagarin wrote: "Exile does not break the ties which bind the heart to the Fatherland." He earnestly sought "a reconciliation between the just demands of universal civilization and of the national spirit." Although a Jesuit and therefore a participant in the Latin rite, he was one of the staunch advocates of the Eastern liturgy. He held that the Russian church must join Rome but that it must preserve "its venerable rites, its ancient discipline, its national liturgy and its physiognomy proper." [5]

Gagarin often expressed regret that in the eyes of so many of his compatriots Catholicism still meant simply Latinism, a faith connected with the political interest of the Poles, Russia's

[5] Gagarin, *op. cit.*

traditional enemies, and therefore representative of an element that was not only alien but actually inimical. He wrote quite explicitly that if this tension were to be released, it was above all necessary that his country's national spirit be respected. Gagarin's Russian friends who visited him in Paris after his ordination carried with them an initial prejudice based on the fact that he had become a Jesuit, for the Jesuits were commonly considered formidable and cunning conspirators against the Orthodox faith: this was the traditional picture retained from the days when the false Demetrius sat on the throne in Moscow among his Catholic courtiers. One of Gagarin's friends, Leskov, relates how surprised he was to find the former prince had retained so many of his native traits: "He was a candid man," writes Leskov, "who did not at all resemble a Jesuit as we commonly represent him to ourselves. . . . Until the end he preserved much of the Russian simplicity of soul." He was "kind, very sensitive and comprehending." [6]

John Gagarin had left Russia under a cloud. There was a personal tragedy in his life which may have led him to enter religion. He had been a friend of Pushkin and belonged to what we might describe as the "fast set," the "dissipated cadets," as Leskov calls them. They were for the most part officers of the guard or young Petersburg dandies like Pushkin, who courted beautiful Petersburg ladies, indulged in wild drinking parties, and fought duels. Their practical jokes were not only imprudent but often cruel and dangerous. These very cadets were the ones suspected of having sent Pushkin the anonymous letter which precipitated the fatal duel. Although the authors of the letter were never discovered, the name of Gagarin was whispered.

Leskov relates that once he mentioned Pushkin's name in Father Gagarin's presence. The latter showed deep agitation and began to weep. He declared that he was eager to clear him-

[6] See Leskov, *Jesuit Gagarin.*

self of this heavy accusation but that after the poet's death, the anonymous letter had been brought to Paris and been hidden away. If only he could get hold of it, he would be able to prove his innocence.

Until today the mystery of the fatal letter has not been solved. Actually Gagarin was in no way involved in the Pushkin affair, but he belonged to that gay, heartless Petersburg set which was responsible for the death of Russia's greatest poet. He was deeply affected by this fact, and Pushkin's memory tormented him all his life.[7] It is thus that Leskov describes him in his moving account full of warm sympathy: a man still deeply attached to his country; a man whose heart had been stricken by Pushkin's tragedy, which is in fact Russia's tragedy.

In Paris, Father Gagarin devoted his energies to the collection and classification of books on Russia. He was actually the founder of the Bibliothèque Slave, the Jesuit library in Paris containing a precious collection of books concerning Russia and the Slavonic peoples. Later, Father Pierling, the learned Jesuit to whom we have already referred, continued the task begun by Father Gagarin, and many Russian scholars, both Catholic and Orthodox, have been able to study Russian history and religion at the Bibliothèque Slave. Thus Father Gagarin, though exiled from his native land, was a promoter of Russian culture abroad.[8]

Petcherin's story is also strange and moving. This man who had spoken of the "sweet hatred of the Fatherland" could never efface its memory from his heart. Wladimir Petcherin had been a young professor of Greek at the Moscow University. He had traveled abroad and visited Belgium. At that time he

[7] Schegolev, the distinguished Russian historian, who made a special study of the circumstances of Pushkin's duel, has definitely proved that Prince John Gagarin was in no way responsible for the fatal anonymous letter. For further details concerning the life and work of Father Gagarin in Paris, see Polonsky, *Unpublished letters of J. Gagarin,* and *Literaturny Arkhiv Russkikh Jesuitov.*

[8] See Polonsky, *Literaturny Arkhiv Russkikh Jesuitov.*

was an unbeliever, one of the humanistic and idealistic atheists we have previously described. He belonged to the radical intelligentsia, and he hated not Russia herself but rather the régime of oppression which she represented in his experience. If he desired her destruction, it was, as he wrote in his poem, because this destruction would be "the sign of a universal revival." Like Bakunin, he believed that Russia would achieve world revolution.

In Brussels the young radical entered a church and talked to a Redemptorist priest whom he met there. He mocked and defied the religious, but the latter started a friendly debate, opposing to the young man's heated attacks the arguments of Christian dogma. As a result, Petcherin was converted and soon afterwards entered the Redemptorist order. When the news reached Russia, he was summoned back. He refused to return and was deprived of his civic rights and property.

Petcherin's order sent him to England and then to Ireland, where he spent twenty years of his life in a Redemptorist community in Limerick. He gained great eminence as a religious because of the austerity of his life and his rare gift of eloquence. His sermons in English have been published in *The Catholic Pulpit,* an anthology of the best English Catholic preaching.

After twenty years of monastic life, Petcherin asked to be relieved of his vows. His request was granted, and he became a secular priest attached to the Mater Misericordia Hospital in Dublin. He filled this post for twenty-three years until his death in 1885. In Dublin, as in Limerick, he was known as a saintly man. However, he must have retained something of his tempestuous disposition. In Ireland he became involved in a conflict with the Protestant population, during the course of which he publicly burned anti-Catholic publications. He was accused of having destroyed the Protestant Bible and was summoned to court. During the trial, he acted as his own attorney for the defense.

The story with regard to the events surrounding Petcherin's

departure from his monastery (perhaps it is only a legend) is very revealing so far as these spiritual émigrés are concerned. It is said that after he had been a monk for twenty-three years he heard a Russian lady in Limerick sing songs of their native land. From that day on, he pined for Russia. His health broke down and he asked to be relieved of his monastic vows. It is under these circumstances that he is presumed to have gone to the Dublin hospital as chaplain.[9]

Indeed it was at about this time that Petcherin's thoughts were tending homeward. But it is probable that his nostalgia was awakened not by a lady singing Russian songs but by the letters he received from Russia. And he received Russian journals, also, which apprised him of the fact that his name had not been forgotten. Two prominent journalists, Katkov and Pogodin, had started a debate concerning Petcherin. Katkov declared that a man of Petcherin's talents should be allowed to return to Russia. Pogodin argued that it would be dangerous to admit him, since he was a highly gifted man who might start a Catholic movement.

Petcherin was naturally deeply moved by this debate. He sent a reply to the Russian papers which is worth quoting, for it reflects his ardent nature and his devotion to truth and justice.

People have strange ideas concerning the so-called conversions to the Catholic faith. The sensitiveness of youth, a sermon, a Catholic priest! Things do not happen that way! My conversion

---

[9] See Gershenson, *Vladimir Petcherin*. In 1932 Gershenson published a diary of Petcherin which he declared to have been recently discovered in the Russian archives. According to this diary, Petcherin experienced a complete disappointment in his religious vocation towards the end of his life. However, we know from his Irish contemporaries that he fulfilled his duties as chaplain with the greatest zeal and devotion. There is no possibility of checking on this diary of Petcherin, but a few years earlier Gershenson published a mystical diary of Peter Chaadaiev which was later proved to be apocryphal. Petcherin's supposed "disappointment" suited the ends of Soviet anti-religious propaganda and was therefore given considerable publicity in the U.S.S.R. Such material should be handled with caution, but we refer to it in order to make our bibliography complete. Concerning the diary see Petcherin, *Zamoguilniya Zapisski*.

began very early: since the first rays of reasonable life, on my native soil, in Russia, far away, in the Russian army. The spectacle of injustice and of an awful lack of conscience in all the branches of Russian life—that was the first sermon which strongly influenced me . . . I like to remember the words of the great Pope Gregory VII: "I was devoted to justice and hated injustice; therefore I die in exile." Let this serve as epigraph to my life and as epitaph after my death.[10]

This hatred of injustice is very typical of Russian Catholics in the nineteenth century. Conversion was not an aristocratic whim; it was motivated by the deep impulse towards a Christian social order. Of course all Russian converts to Catholicism were not socially minded. There were those who were exclusively concerned with the development of the inner man and who found in Catholicism a means of attaining it. But there were many who, like Petcherin, participated in the movement for the emancipation of Russia's oppressed, and to whom the social aspects of the Catholic Church were of paramount importance. In his reply to the Russian press, Petcherin quite clearly stated where his sympathies lay:

Mr. Pogodin very naively forbids my entry into Russia. He is quite right! If, as a result of some great transformation, the doors of my fatherland opened before me, I declare in advance, that I side not with the old Russia, but with the new one; even today I extend with fervent sympathy my hand to the new generation, to beloved Russian youth and would like to embrace them in the name of freedom of conscience and of the national council [meaning a representative régime].[11]

We can now understand what it was that Petcherin hated in Russia. It was not the fatherland but the oppressive and retrogressive autocracy, the restrictions imposed on man's thought and conscience. The chaplain who succeeded him at

[10] Quoted from Gershenson's *Vladimir Petcherin.*
[11] *Ibid.*

the Dublin hospital and who had known him intimately, relates that Petcherin valued every memory attached to Russia. In his will, he requested that all his books and papers should be sent to the Moscow university.

Even those Russian Catholics who did not profess liberal ideas or were not directly concerned with Russia's social problem still retain something of that social spirit and express it in their lives and writings. Father John Gagarin stated in his works that if Russia did not admit the influence of the stream of universal civilization she would be carried away by the revolutionary movement. Like Bakunin, he predicted that this revolution would be terrible.

Prince Demetrius Galitzin, the least Russian of these Russian Catholics, was not aware of his country's social and political problems. In the colony of Loretto (Maryland) which he had founded, he was entirely engrossed in the affairs of his parish. But this American pioneer had more than one characteristic in common with the Seekers of Silence. He practiced kenotic Christianity. His Russian property having been confiscated, he lived in great poverty and wore "patched clothes." The debts he contracted in order to build up his colony weighed heavily on him, and he swore that he would never ride in a carriage until he had paid them off. So he drove in a sleigh in winter and in summer. An old engraving represents him in this extraordinary conveyance, wrapped in his shabby greatcoat.[12] As in the case of the Russian contemplatives, his Loretto was a "desert" in which he devoted himself to the poor.

The man who, along with Petcherin, best expresses the Russian Catholics' social aspirations was Michael Lunin, the Decembrist. In his youth, Lunin was one of the cadets of Petersburg society, serving as an officer in a crack-regiment of the cavalry. He was an expert pistol shot and like Pushkin he fought many duels. During Napoleon's invasion of Russia, Lunin was sent to the front, where he displayed great courage.

[12] See Lemcke, *Life and Work of Prince Demetrius Augustine Gallitzine.*

Once in the thick of battle, observing that an infantry regiment had wavered, he dismounted and took command of the men, marching before them in his dazzling white uniform, an easy target for the enemy's bullets. He was known to be absolutely fearless. On his country estate he would set out unaccompanied, armed only with a wooden prong (the primitive peasant weapon), to hunt a bear.

Lunin went to Paris with Alexander's armies. Here his imagination was fired with the ideals of the French Revolution, which he carried back to Russia. Having resigned from the army, he returned to France and lived in great poverty, giving lessons in Russian and copying manuscripts. In Paris, he met the French socialist St. Simon and became his fervent disciple. And it was also in Paris that he was subsequently converted to Catholicism. When he returned to Russia he joined the Decembrist movement.

Lunin called himself a citizen of the world. He was bitterly opposed to autocracy and serfdom: "We want the freedom of will, the freedom of thought, the freedom of action!" he declared. After the suppression of the Decembrist uprising, he was condemned to twenty years of hard labor in Siberia. Thus he shared the fate of that remarkable Russian nineteenth-century élite who gave up their own hopes for the future in order to make their contribution to man's emancipation. He left a diary which shows the depth of his spiritual life.[13]

One could hardly describe Michael Lunin as a fanciful aristocrat or a denationalized Russian. He is typical of his Russian contemporaries: a dreamer and an ascetic, an ardent searcher after truth, a courageous champion of freedom. But like Petcherin he realized that a more equitable social order could not be attained through godless methods. In Christian universality they both saw the hope of their fatherland and of the world.

[13] See Lunin, *Works and Letters* (with annotations by Streich). See also Hessen and Kogan, *Dekabrist Lunin*.

XI

Chaadaiev

WE HAVE SEEN the Russian Catholics dispersed throughout France, England, and America, spiritual exiles torn between their religion and the land they left behind them. As we return to Russia to look more closely at this complex scene in her history, we discern the solitary figure of a man who, although he never became a Catholic, looked upon Russia's detachment from the stem of Christian culture as the source of her social and spiritual maladies. One of the most brilliant thinkers of his time, he broadened the spiritual horizons of his contemporaries and left a deep imprint on Russian culture. This man is Peter Chaadaiev.

Pushkin, who was Chaadaiev's intimate friend, was the author of the following epigram concerning him.

> Born by the supreme will of the gods
> In the chains of the Tsar's service,
> He would have been Brutus in Rome, in Athens—Pericles
> Here he is officer of the hussars.[1]

Chaadaiev was one of the dissipated cadets of his time. He fought courageously against Napoleon and accompanied the tsar on his "fabulous campaign." He, too, was famous for his duels, and as the member of a Masonic lodge, he was drawn into the current of humanism. He was known to be friendly with the Decembrists, and consequently he was treated as a suspect by the authorities. Like Lunin, he was known for his absolute fearlessness. His reputation as a soldier was so high

[1] Written by Pushkin on Chaadaiev's portrait.

that when, on one occasion, he refused to fight a duel, his brother officers approved his inaction, declaring that Chaadaiev's courage was above suspicion.

After the war Chaadaiev was aide-de-camp to Prince Vassiltchikov, the Governor-General of Petersburg. At that time he made friends with Pushkin, who was still a student in the Imperial Lyceum, a school for young noblemen founded by the tsars. Chaadaiev was the first to guess that this turbulent, curly-headed boy might become Russia's greatest poetical genius. Together the two young men participated in the cadets' drinking parties and attended secret meetings where "revolution" was the topic of discussion. Chaadaiev strongly influenced young Pushkin. The hussar officer was a man of erudition; he inspired the poet with the love of culture as well as with the "subversive" ideas brought back from Paris.

Nevertheless Chaadaiev was not a radical. He was ambitious and worldly, and he seemed to be destined for a brilliant military career. This career was unexpectedly broken off when, as Vassiltchikov's aide-de-camp, he was dispatched to Emperor Alexander's headquarters at Troppau, where the tsar was conferring with Metternich. The mission entrusted to Chaadaiev was a most unpleasant one. He was to report to his sovereign concerning a revolt which had broken out in Petersburg among the soldiers of one of the regiments of the guard. It was a foregone conclusion that when the tsar became aware of the rebellion the subversive regiment would be disbanded and its officers, all of whom were Chaadaiev's friends, would incur severe penalties. Whatever his duties as a soldier, he could not but sympathize with the offenders.

Chaadaiev left for Troppau as he was told, but he dallied on his way, lost a few hours changing into full dress uniform, and presented himself before the tsar after a considerable delay. The interview took place behind closed doors, and it was rumored that it did not start as a friendly meeting although Alexander is said to have shown no ill temper; at the end of the conversation, he even became quite cordial. The tsar discussed the capital's political atmosphere with the young aide-de-camp and dismissed him with the promise of a very desirable promotion in the near future.[2]

Chaadaiev returned to Petersburg in great disquietude. He was to be promoted while his brother officers were to be punished for their rebellion. Feeling that his position was untenable, he sent to the tsar his resignation from the army.

After this incident, which had deeply affected him, Chaadaiev lived in retirement for several years, suffering, it was rumored, from acute hypochondria. He studied a great deal, received no visitors, cut himself off entirely from social life. For a time he traveled abroad, visiting France, England, and Germany, where he made the acquaintance of the philosopher Schelling. On his return to Russia he took up residence in Moscow. His doctor, finding him in a state of deep depression, advised him to resume his former social life. Why should he not go to the club, where so many friends had been inquiring for him?

Chaadaiev went to the club. He enjoyed his first visit and subsequently became a frequent guest. Soon he was invited to the various literary salons. He took society by storm, not as the reckless cadet of old but as a grave philosopher. At that time he was thirty-seven years old, tall, handsome, immaculately dressed. His pale face and bald head seemed chiseled from marble. A faint, half-ironical, half-indulgent smile hovered about his thin lips. His brilliant repartees, his eloquence and culture, became proverbial. Men admired him, women worshipped him.

"Will it seem strange to you," wrote a young girl, "if I request your blessing? I have often wished to do so, and if I asked of you this favor, I would be happy to receive it on my knees." The girl was Avdotia Narova, a romantic and sickly

[2] Chaadaiev, according to the tsar's promise, was to be appointed personal aide-de-camp to His Majesty.

PETER CHAADAIEV

young woman whom Chaadaiev had met on his aunt's country estate, during the period of his retirement. Although he had many friends, Avdotia was to be the only romance of his life. She died young, and Chaadaiev, who survived her by many years, asked to be buried at her side.

Towards other women, he showed interest, even solicitude, but he soon forgot them. A certain Mrs. Panova [3] once wrote to remind him that he had left her previous letter, in which she had confided her doubts about her faith and asked his advice, unanswered. Chaadaiev sat down to write a reply to this note. He wrote not one but several letters, and it took him many days. But when he finished them, he did not post them. The lady in question never knew that he had written her a reply. Indeed it is probable that Chaadaiev forgot his object in writing soon after having begun his task, but as the result of this accident the ideas which had long awaited expression took form in one of the most remarkable essays in Russian literature, *The Philosophical Letters*.

Chaadaiev showed his manuscript to some friends, who re-copied and circulated it in the city. The editor of a Moscow journal published it. *The Philosophical Letters* led to heated and even violent debates; they stimulated Russian thought for nearly a century. Nicholas I thought them so dangerous that he ordered the editor who published them to be deported and the journal itself to be suppressed. Chaadaiev was declared insane and placed under medical supervision.

Literary critics, historians, and theologians have pondered over *The Philosophical Letters*. Orthodox writers and Catholic scholars have scrutinized every line.[4] Father John Gagarin published them in Paris, where Soloviev read them, jotting

[3] According to another version, the lady in question was Mrs. Levashova, Chaadaiev's great friend and admirer, in whose house he lived in Moscow.

[4] The most exhaustive work on Chaadaiev is by Charles Quenet, a priest attached to the chancery of the Archbishop of Paris. See Quenet, *Tchaadaev et les Lettres Philosophiques*.

down marginal comments. The copy with Soloviev's notes is preserved at the Slavonic library founded in Paris by Father Pierling. Later, the Russian critic Gershenson published a new revised edition, and more recently still, Soviet research workers have added much new material as yet unknown to the public. The fact that such patient and meticulous scholarship has been devoted to *The Philosophical Letters* indicates their value in the judgment of both Eastern and Western critics. Indeed, Chaadaiev raised, in his "Letters" and in another essay, *The Apology of a Madman*, written a few years later, the questions fundamental to the study of Russian cultural and political development.

These essays embody a religious approach to both culture and history. Chaadaiev was a learned and well read man. Both at home and during his journey abroad, he studied Western thought, especially the philosophy of history. He was well acquainted with Western religious writers and was influenced by the French Catholic thinkers Bonnalde and Joseph de Maistre, who had inspired the Russian Catholics. His political outlook was modified by the spirit of his time. Not that he was an active revolutionary. He remained attached to monarchy even after he had suffered from tsarist censorship, for he had too keen a sense of the true function of authority, of order and harmony, to be a rebel. Yet he did certainly belong to the number of the "protesting one." He, too, considered the régime then existing in Russia oppressive and retrogressive. He denounced slavery and obscurantism, keenly aware that if social injustice continued to prevail, his country would be shaken by a terrible upheaval. "Socialism," he wrote, "will triumph not because it is right but because we are wrong."

However, Chaadaiev was not so much concerned with the social and political problem as with the ethical and religious one. He believed that Russia had been reduced to a state of complacency because she was not animated by a true religious spirit. Some of his accusations are as bitter as those of Petcherin. If he did not hate the fatherland, neither did he hesitate to uncover its wounds. He wrote:

Look at all the space we occupy, and you will find not a single bright memory. . . . We live in the present alone, in its most narrow limits, without a past and without a future, in a state of dead stagnation. Ideas of duty, right, justice, live in Europe. She has built the temple of civilization.[5]

Meanwhile, he felt, Russia was drifting on ebbing waters; she was a bleak, barren country where the fruit of Christianity had not ripened. These are truly harsh words of condemnation. Today, after all that Russian culture has produced, after the rich blossoming of her intellectual powers, we cannot accept Chaadaiev's judgment. But it was the mood prevalent in the Russia of his day: the foundation was already being laid for the methods of autocriticism applied by the Russians. Men like Herzen, Petcherin, and Bakunin saw the root of evil in the political deadlock of Nicholas' régime. Chaadaiev gave it a religious and moral interpretation.

The author of *The Philosophical Letters* sees Europe's development as a process closely linked with the development of Christianity. Mankind has grown up and built its temple of civilization in the light of Christianity, which is the manifestation of a universal spirit. As the consequence of the Schism Russia had been cut off from this universal stream, and the fruit of Christianity had therefore not ripened in Russia. Universal Christianity, headed by the Pope, had "centralized Christian ideas and bound them together," while Russia remained withdrawn from the sources of spiritual fertility.

In so far as the "Letters" touch upon Mrs. Panova's specific problems, Chaadaiev does not advise her to abandon Orthodoxy. Nor did he himself wish to do so. He asserts that the surest way of leading a life of perfection is to follow the reli-

[5] Chaadaiev, *Philosophical Letters*, No. 1.

gious teachings and traditions in which one has been brought up. Yet he writes, concerning Catholicism:

A teaching founded on the supreme principle of *unity* and the direct transmission of truth through its successive servants of course corresponds most of all to the true spirit of religion: for it can be reduced to the fusion of all existing moral forces into one idea, one feeling, and to the gradual establishment of a social system which must restore the kingdom of truth among men. All other teachings, by the very fact of their separation from the initial doctrine, disprove in advance the exalted words of the Savior: "Keep them in Thy name whom Thou hast given Me: that they may be one as We are also" (St. John, XVII, II).[6]

Nicholas I called *The Philosophical Letters* a "mixture of insolent absurdities worthy of a madman." Herzen spoke of them enthusiastically as "a shot fired in the darkness of night." The radicals interpreted Chaadaiev's essay as a bold call to liberation, an attempt to cleanse the stifling atmosphere of Nicholas's Russia. But they disregard the historical and religious concepts which the writer expressed. Herzen's positivism prevented him from abstracting their profound metaphysical principles.

The religious essence of this work was grasped by critics belonging to the spiritual-minded intelligentsia, but they were deeply attached to Orthodoxy and were shocked by Chaadaiev's inclinations towards Catholic universality. A heated controversy ensued. At that time the ban on the philosopher was partially lifted. The doctor who had been ordered to visit him regularly in order to "check up on his mental condition" was a kindly and liberal man who made friends with his "patient." The legend of Chaadaiev's insanity could not long be maintained, and once more he resumed his literary activities.

Chaadaiev lived in an old Moscow mansion which had been offered him by his friends, the Levashov family. It was a musty

[6] *Ibid.,* No. 2.

building badly in need of repairs, which seemed about to crumble. The philosopher was continually in debt. He, too, practiced kenotic Christianity, but much against his will and chiefly as the consequence of the bad management of his country estate. Even under such adverse circumstances, however, he remained the fastidious gentleman of bygone days. He was "at home" on Mondays, and most of his illustrious contemporaries visited the old house—Herzen, Gogol, Granovsky, the brilliant professor who had brought German philosophy to the Moscow university, and the distinguished foreigners who came to Russia, such as Berlioz and Prosper Mérimée.

When Chaadaiev appeared in Moscow's literary salons he was, as the French Ambassador Pozzo di Borgo describes him, "the perfectly bred Russian gentleman." Gershenson says that he was "beloved by the best men of two or three generations." [7] and the poet Tiutchev who, being deeply opposed to Catholicism, was Chaadaiev's violent opponent, declared that he loved him "more than anyone else." But there was always a mysterious aloofness in this tall, slender figure clothed in immaculate dark clothes and wearing the soldier's cross for bravery on his chest. As he stood silent, leaning against a pillar, he appeared, according to one of his contemporaries, "as a living protest." And Herzen writes: "God knows why, men were intimidated by his motionless face, his piercing gaze, his sad smile, his sarcastic condescension." [8]

Some of Chaadaiev's ideas resemble those of Yury Krijanitch. Like the Croatian scholar, the author of *The Philosophical Letters* believed that he had a mission to fulfil and that this mission was Russia's enlightenment. He was not aware that his concept of world history and of Russia's destinies would arouse a storm. On the contrary, he thought that he would stimulate Russian culture and become the leading spirit of a revival. He requested Count Benckendorff (Pushkin's censor)

[7] Gershenson, *Jizni Mishlenie Chaadaieva*.
[8] Herzen, *Biloie i Dumy*.

to transmit a letter addressed to the Emperor. In this letter Chaadaiev suggested that he should be appointed "adviser and philosopher" to the state. Count Benckendorff coldly discouraged him, saying that he did not dare to show the letter to His Majesty. This incident reminds us of the Croat's desire to become "court librarian" and adviser to Tsar Alexis.

The *Politica* of Yury Krijanitch and *The Philosophical Letters* of Chaadaiev have certain characteristics in common: both stress the historiosophical outlook: both consider the evolution of mankind to be directed by divine providence. But since he was a Russian of social position, Chaadaiev exercised a far deeper influence on the thinking of his day than had the adventurous Slav missionary. The French writer Marquis de Custine, who visited Russia at that time, describes him as the most distinguished figure in Russian intellectual circles. Pushkin's fame is closely linked with that of Chaadaiev. It was under the latter's guidance that the poet began his literary career. Chaadaiev furnished inspiration for Pushkin's first revolutionary poems, of which the *Ode to Liberty* is an example:

> Alas, wherever I cast my glance
> I behold everywhere scourges and chains
> The deathly shame of the laws
> The helpless tears of slavery.

And in his *Epistle to Chaadaiev* Pushkin wrote that "the star of happiness" would some day rise for them both:

> Russia will awaken from sleep
> And will write our names
> On the ruins of autocracy.

The two friends were to liberate Russia together. Instead, Pushkin was banished to the southern steppes and Chaadaiev became a philosopher. The poet in exile warmly remembered the friend, "always a sage and sometimes a dreamer," [9] who had restored "hope and peace" in the most tragic days of his life.

[9] Pushkin, *Epistle to Chaadaiv.*

XII

The Slavophiles

IT TOOK A long time for the storm aroused by *The Philosophical Letters* to subside. Their author was still the object of the tsar's displeasure. Writers, journalists, literary critics attached to Russia's historical traditions, accused Chaadaiev of being unpatriotic. The Orthodox treated him as a renegade. The poet Yazykov wrote that he was the "disobedient son of honorable parents" and that he had "kissed the Pope's slipper." He was nicknamed "the little *abbé*." But the most serious attacks were made by Khomiakov, the leader of the Slavophiles.

Chaadaiev may be said to have acted as a catalyst. He stimulated not only the activities of his sympathizers but also those of his opponents. In reaction to his bitter criticism of Russia's past, Slavophile ideology, which was then in the making, took definite shape. Chaadaiev even made a positive contribution to its development by his second essay, *The Apology of a Madman*, the title of which was an ironic reference to the tsar's verdict with regard to the writer's sanity.

In *The Apology of a Madman* Chaadaiev maintained that Russia's past was dark and barren, but he admitted that the future was still in her hands. Like Krijanitch, he believed that the nations were successively called upon to be the exponents of an idea and that in her day Russia would serve as the vessel of election. The Russians represent a blank page in history; they have a "virgin mind" which will receive the imprint of a new ideology. "If they have come after the others, it is to do betters than the others. . . . I have the intimate conviction that we are called to solve most of the social problems, to complete most of the ideas originated in the old societies: we are called to state our opinion on the gravest questions which absorb mankind."

Thus the author finally expresses his belief in Russia's special mission, which since the days of the Third Rome had been the guiding principle of Russian historiosophy. But he still lays emphasis on the fact that his country must receive enlightenment from the West before she can fulfil her vocation. Addressing himself to the Slavophiles, he reproaches them with having evolved a vague and misty ideology and requests that they formulate clearly their views on Russia's future.

In reaction to Chaadaiev's indictment the leaders of the Slavophile school developed the idea of Russia's special mission according to strict Orthodox doctrine. They placed themselves on the religious ground chosen by the philosopher, but they sought to prove that light came not from the West but from the East, and revealed itself in the Christianity which was innately Russian.

Among the Slavophile leaders the most outstanding was the layman Alexis Khomiakov, who is accredited by the modern Orthodox not only as a philosopher but as a theologian. Like most of the young noblemen of his time, Khomiakov began his career as a soldier and served in a hussar regiment of the guard. He fought in the Turkish campaign of 1828; later he retired from the army and led the life of a country gentleman.

Even as a young man, Khomiakov revealed a deeply religious spirit. He practiced Orthodoxy scrupulously, attending religious services, observing fasts, and wearing the heaviest soldier's equipment as a means of mortification. When he retired to his estate he led a happy home life, was unpretentious and sober in his habits, and held himself aloof from the political turmoil of his time. He was a very cultured, and even a learned, man skilled in so many pursuits both intellectual and practical that he has been called a universal mind: he was an experienced farmer, a good huntsman, an expert chemist and engineer who constructed machines and invented mechanical conveniences as a hobby. And he wrote brilliant prose and was a talented poet. Together with his friends Constantine Aksakov and the brothers Kireievsky and Yury Samarin, he evolved the Slavophile doctrine.

As we have seen, this doctrine rejected Western cultural trends and did not admit the benefits of the reforms effected by Peter the Great. It asserted that Russia's development had its own original pattern and that her ancient traditions were the proper guides of her creativeness. The Slavophiles considered Russian Orthodoxy the great wellspring of these traditions; yet they were not the champions of theocracy. They were in fact hostile to any kind of organized power. Khomiakov was a religious anarchist who asserted that the existence of state institutions was deplored by the Russian people, who considered the exercise of force unjust. Rather than be themselves its instruments, they *delegated* the prerogative to the tsar, who thus "assumed the sin of violence."

Chaadaiev has been accused of having painted a gloomy picture of Russian history, but Khomiakov was no less pessimistic. He was pitiless in revealing what he called "Russia's sins in the past": ignorance, internecine strife, corruption, the arbitrary decrees of the ruling class, the bondage of the state church, the clergy's obscurantism and spiritual sloth. "There was nothing worthy in Russia," writes Khomiakov, almost repeating Chaadaiev's words, "it was a chaos of blood and mud. . . . There was not a single happy moment in the people's life." [1]

Khomiakov believed that it was from this long-suffering people that the light would come. The MIR, or agricultural commune, was the perfect type of society based on a Christian social order (an idea which we have seen to be common to most

[1] Khomiakov, *The Church.*

Russian thinkers of the time). As to Orthodoxy, it was inherent
not in the state church but in the Mystical Body. Orthodoxy
was informed by the law of love, which eluded all bondage
and all physical organization. It needed no superimposed
authority, no *magister*; it did not even have to be governed by
an ecumenical council. The principle of Orthodoxy was *sobornost*, the ecumenical spirit of the people. This *sobornost*, this
bond of love through the Holy Ghost, *was* the church.

Thus the Slavophiles opposed Orthodoxy, the religion of the
untrammeled spirit, to Catholicism, which they called a "juridical" faith based more on Roman law than on the divine
commandment of love. They were deeply hostile to Rome.
The essential mistake in their position was, as Berdiaev justly
points out, that they oppose to the Western historical church,
that is, to an earthly organization, a mystical *ideal* church of
the East which is actually a metaphysical concept. Berdiaev
adds that the Slavophiles knew nothing about the interior
aspect of the Catholic Church, its mystical and sacramental
life. They criticized Catholicism for what they called its legal-
ism, but "to criticize Catholicism," he concludes, "often leads
to Protestantism." [2] Indeed, Khomiakov's concept of authority
inclines towards the Protestant outlook. Many Russian Orthodox, though accepting Khomiakov's theology, do not follow
him in his doctrine concerning the nature of the church.

Russian cultural circles now possessed a definite national and
religious doctrine which refuted Chaadaiev's contention that
Russia's light must come from the West. The author of *The
Philosophical Letters* was himself impressed by Khomiakov's
writings. There was much in this exalted concept of Russia, of
her mission, of her ecumenical spirit of love which attracted
him. He even translated one of Khomiakov's articles and sent
it to a Catholic friend in France, the Count de Gircourt, who
was interested in Russian spirituality.

Slavophilism stimulated interest in research work devoted to

[2] Berdiaev, *Alexei Khomiakov*.

Russia's present and past. Historical and geographical essays on the Russian Empire were published. There was a new interest in folklore and popular music. Yet the Slavophiles displeased the authorities of church and state almost as much as had Chaadaiev. The Slavophiles, too, were considered dangerous, since their religious anarchism was as subversive as Chaadaiev's avowed preference for European civilization. The Slavophile's definition of the nature of the Church involved the rejection not only of Rome but also of the Russian official Church. This very indifference to political problems awakened suspicion. When a group of revolutionaries were arrested in Petersburg, the police were surprised that no disciples of Khomiakov were among those apprehended. "But of course!", a high official exclaimed, "The Slavophiles are so deep, they never get caught."

After Khomiakov's death the Slavophile movement degenerated; actually it became, with its new leader Katkov, a retrogressive and narrowly nationalistic school which had little in common with the original populist trend and was denounced by Wladimir Soloviev as "zoological nationalism." From that day on, high officials regarded it with favor, while the Russian intelligentsia indignantly abandoned it. Dostoievsky describes this degeneration as "reducing God to an attribute of nationality," to the "old commonplaces ground out in all the Slavophile mills in Moscow." Nevertheless for the duration of its integrity, Slavophilism had made itself felt (to use another of Dostoievsky's expressions) as "a perfectly new saying, the last word, the sole word of renewal" which gave Russian religious thought a new impulse.

In his essay on Orthodox ecclesiology Father Congar, the French Dominican, examines Khomiakov's doctrine from the Catholic point of view. He points out that this doctrine has simply stressed certain aspects of the church and omitted others. Catholic dogma also conceives of the church as a communion of love through the Holy Ghost, as the Mystical Body of

Christ. The unity of the Catholic Church is effected by a bond of brotherhood "animated by the spirit of the Lord." If at certain times this inner aspect has been neglected in the West, the Catholic Church today "seeks more than ever to live and think along these fundamental lines."

"But," Father Congar concludes, "if we retain as do the Orthodox, the entire positive substance of this ecclesiology, we add something to it, or rather, we believe that the Orthodox subtract something from it. What we add and what they subtract is the element of the militant Church, the realities which are developed in the Church of Jesus Christ, its condition of Church *on earth,* of a Church made *ex hominibus* and not *ex angelis.*" [3]

Wladimir Soloviev, who in his youth was closely linked to the original Slavophile movement and was later disappointed in it, gives a striking illustration of the principles which Father Congar seeks to convey. He relates the old Russian legend of St. Nicholas and St. Cassien.

One day as the two saints were journeying along a country road, they saw a cart and horse bogged down in the mud. "Let us give a hand to the driver," St. Nicholas suggested, but St. Cassien shook his head. "If we soil our garments," he objected, "we shall not be able to enter paradise!" But without heeding his companion, St. Nicholas waded into the mud and helped the driver to pull out his cart. And, sure enough, his garments became badly soiled.

When the saints reached the gates of paradise St. Peter saw that St. Nicholas' garments were soiled, while those of St. Cassien were dazzling white. But it was St. Nicholas who received all the honors for the work he had accomplished on earth. [4]

To the Western mind Khomiakov's doctrine will appear

---

[3] Congar, *Chrétiens Désunis: Principes d'un "Oecumenisme" Catholique.*

[4] Soloviev, *La Russie et l'Église Universelle.*

strange and even somewhat bewildering. Yet it contained the dynamism which official Orthodoxy lacked. It gave a bold and illuminating interpretation of Russia's essential mysticism, which consisted in the apprehension of truth by religious intuition rather than by rational dogmatic concepts. This intuitiveness had as its corollary the necessity of spiritual autonomy. As we have seen, it characterized the Russian religious temper from the very beginning.

Khomiakov's ideas concerning the Russian ecumenical spirit, what he calls *sobornost*, are extremely interesting. *Sobornost* animates not only the Church but the laity, all the Christian people of Russia; it is a bond of fraternity between all men inasmuch as they are members of the Mystical Body.

The indisputable merit of the Slavophiles is that they sought to replace the lifeless mechanism of the state by a living organism, the soul of the people. Their social ideology is opposed not only to the autocracy of their own day but also to the Marxist state. Their grounds for conflict with the godless socialists of their time were more real than any of their differences with Chaadaiev. Though they were zealous opponents of the latter, they borrowed much from his teaching, and they held with him the concept of a Christian world order.

The Slavophile problem is intricate and can scarcely be treated fully in this chapter. But for those who want to grasp the soul of Russia it is essential to know the elements of this doctrine. The great dispute between the Slavophiles and the Westerners went on long after the deaths of Khomiakov and Chaadaiev. It is still going on. Will the light come to Russia from the East or from the West? Such is the question reiterated in the Russian mind with ghostly insistence. This haunting quality is no doubt resident in the fact that the problem is in its nature insoluble. It is best to say, with Yury Krijanitch, that Russia stands between East and West and is called to form a bond between them.

Once more we shall refer to Dostoievsky, who was the man

most deeply aware of Russia's mission in the world and who firmly believed that she was to say a "new word." Dostoievsky spoke of Pushkin's call to universality. He said that the West was "a land of holy miracles" and that "every Russian" had "two homes: Russia and Europe."

XIII

The Search of God

ONE NIGHT in the year 1849 the members of a political circle met in Petersburg, at the home of their leader, Petrashevsky. Here a young writer named Fedor Dostoievsky read aloud the famous letter of Bielinsky to Gogol, in which Bielinsky wrote that Russia "presented the terrible spectacle of a land where men sold other men as slaves" and which was governed "by an immense corporation of thieves and plunderers." Because Gogol was one of the supporters of the official church, Bielinsky had denounced him as "the defender of the knout, the apostle of ignorance and obscurantism, the panegyrist of Mongol morals." [1]

The meeting was surprised by the police, and Dostoievsky, who actually was in no way connected with politics, was arrested with the other members of the group and condemned to death. At the last moment, when he was standing on the scaffold, he was reprieved. It is this experience which he describes in *The Idiot*.

There were crowds of people, there was noise and shouting; ten thousand faces, ten thousand eyes—all that he had to bear, and worst of all the thought: they are ten thousand, but not one of them is being executed, and I am to be executed. . . . It's strange that people rarely faint in these last moments. On the contrary, the brain is extraordinarily lively and must be working at a tremendous rate. I fancy there is a continual throbbing of

[1] *Obrazovanie,* No. 2 (II), No. 3 (II), "Gogol i Bielinsky," St. Petersburg, 1902.

ideas of all sorts, always unfinished and perhaps absurd, quite irrelevant ideas. . . . Paint the scaffold so that only the last step can be distinctly seen in the foreground, and the criminal having just stepped on it; his head, his face as white as paper; the priest holding up the cross, the man eagerly putting forward his blue lips and looking—and aware of everything. The cross and the head, that's the picture. The priest's face and the executioner's, his two attendants and a few heads and eyes below might be painted in the background, in half light, as the setting.[2]

This is, therefore, not only an extraordinarily haunting picture, as direct and vivid as the set of a film. It is also the account of an ordeal of Dostoievsky's own life that produced a psychic trauma from which he never entirely recovered.

It has been said that the author of *The Brothers Karamazov* was a martyr to the literary profession. Indeed, his life was one of acute and continual suffering. After his narrow escape from execution, which had left him deeply shaken, he was deported to Siberia, where he spent four years at hard labor followed by a period of five years during which he was still prevented from returning to Russia.

"I am almost in despair," he wrote at that time. "It is difficult to express how much I have suffered. Those four years I look upon as a time of living burial. . . . The suffering was inexhaustible." Yet he accepted it with great meekness. "This is my cross," he said, "and I deserve it." During those years of constant suffering, Dostoievsky discovered the true Christian way of life. When he was on his way to prison, he received a New Testament from a woman who had pity on him as he trudged along with his companions in fetters. This book was for him not only a source of comfort but a revelation. Rays of evangelic light permeated his subsequent creative work.

From the Siberian prison Dostoievsky brought back a masterpiece, *The Recollections of the House of the Dead*, his convict's diary. The first ordeal was over, but it was soon fol-

[2] Dostoievsky, *The Idiot*, p. 59.

lowed by others: poverty, sickness, the throes of epilepsy which afflicted him from youth but grew more serious after his terrible experience; debts taken over from his brother added to his own obligations; the struggle to feed himself and his family; the strenuous work imposed on him by his publishers, which taxed him almost beyond human endurance—all these were the crosses of Dostoievsky's life.

None of these crosses impeded his work of creation. It flowed in spite of sickness, indigence, anxiety. Dostoievsky wrote under continual pressure and produced one great work after another: *The Recollections of the House of the Dead* and *The Injured and the Oppressed* were followed by *Crime and Punishment*. Forced to leave Russia to escape imprisonment for debt, he fled abroad and wrote *The Idiot* and *The Possessed*. In 1878, living once more in Petersburg, he began work on *The Brothers Karamazov*. In 1880 he made his famous speech on Pushkin which, as the French critic Melchior de Vogué remarked, "rallied the heart of Russia."

Dostoievsky died a year later and his coffin was accompanied to its last resting place by forty thousand people. His prestige during those last years was immense. He was a medium of expression for the people's very soul, its "incarnation" (as he had written of Pushkin). Indeed one might say that Pushkin's unfinished message, his undeciphered new word, was spoken by Dostoievsky. He was aware of this. Speaking of the enthusiasm of his readers, he wrote to one of his correspondents:

This has been expressed to me by them, from many places, in individual declarations and by whole bodies of them. They have already declared that from me alone they expect a sincere and sympathetic word, and that myself alone they consider as their *leading writer*.[3]

Nevertheless he was without personal or literary vanity. In his greatness as in his suffering, he was a humble man. He was not

[3] Dostoievsky, *Letters and Reminiscences*.

a philosopher like Chaadaiev, seeking to guide the tsar, nor, like Tolstoy, did he seek to persuade the world of the truth he had discovered. Dostoievsky experienced truth immediately in catastrophic shocks. It came to him clothed in fire and tears. It could not be codified but could only be translated in its immediacy, to burn the hearts of men.

Like St. Paul, Dostoievsky could have said that he had been given "a sting of the flesh" and was "transported out of the mind." The epileptic fits from which he suffered deeply afflicted his body and obscured his reason. But they opened the doors of his subconscious mind. In brief snatches, as he himself relates in *The Idiot*, the supernatural world was revealed to him. He knew an ecstasy which he compares to the "last quarter of a second before the fallen pitcher of Mahomet has had time to empty itself." Time stops, and there is eternity: it is "as if something had been torn asunder."

A bliss which would be impossible in an ordinary condition. . . . I feel a perfect harmony in myself and the whole world, and this feeling is so strong and delightful that for some seconds of this rapture you might give ten years of your life.[4]

Dostoievsky also knew the abandonment of sin, the "depths of Satan." Man's corruption, the unfathomable abysses of temptation, the fury of passion, were disclosed to him. The vision was terrifying, but he did not recoil from it. "Love man in his sin," Staretz Zossima taught. And so Dostoievsky painted the great sinners like Stavroguin, Svidrigailov, and the older Karamazov, the "insect-men" full of lust and passion. He painted the collective sin of *The Possessed*. He predicted that Russia would undergo "the temptation of bread and power," of a godless social teaching. In *The Possessed* he described all the sins to be committed by the Bolshevists.

This penetrating insight into the abyss did not lead Dostoievsky to pessimism. He is possibly the least pessimistic of Rus-

[4] *The Idiot*, p. 214.

sian writers, for he had a deep consciousness that man was saved. It can be truly said that his novels are written in strict accordance with the Christian plan of redemption. Dostoievsky's religious concepts were not academic. They were rooted in genuine experience: in the psychic trauma produced by his ordeal on the scaffold and the ineradicable impressions derived from his incarceration in "the house of the dead." This is how he describes the first service he attended in the prison chapel:

We stood in a dense group [like the other prisoners, he was fettered and dressed as a convict]. . . . I remember that I actually liked this: a kind of subtle strange feeling of gratification! "Since it must be!" I thought. The prisoners prayed very fervently and each of them brought his beggar's mite for a taper. . . . We communicated at the early mass. When the priest, with the cup in his hands, read the words: "Are ye come out as against a thief," almost all rolled on the ground, clattering their fetters and seeming to think that the words were literally meant for them.[5]

Indeed, during these four years of living burial, Dostoievsky had drunk at the very sources of Russian life; he had become a new man through the people. He "went to the people" in the truest sense; he was really *one* with them, with the very poorest and most forsaken. The Siberian prison was full of humble peasant folk, deeply and candidly attached to their faith. Dostoievsky wore their clothes and shared their fetters. More than anyone else he had the right to speak for them.

There is so much to be said about Dostoievsky (as about Pushkin) that the meaning of his new word has yet to be fully disclosed. He was a Slavophile and expressed in his novels and in his author's diary an exalted concept of Russia's national genius. Yet he had, as we have seen, a real sense of universality, of the bond of brotherhood and love which bound Russia to Europe, and in fact to the whole world. He conceived the

[5] Quoted from Merejkovsky, *Tolstoy as Man and Artist*.

Russian as an "all-man." It is this sense of universality that enabled him to produce masterpieces intelligible to the whole cultural world. Yet his Orthodoxy, his populism, his profound attachment to his native culture make him typically Russian.

Can Dostoievsky's message be summed up? We hardly think so, and we shall not attempt it. He spoke of a "world saturated with tears from the crust to the core," of men torn between God and diabolical pride, of the temptations of power and of passion. And he also spoke of redemption and of the greatest sinner's being able to ease his heart before God, as did Raskolnikov in *Crime and Punishment.*

There are certain themes which we can follow throughout Dostoievsky's works, a certain key to the main problems which he presents to the reader. Although his narratives appear morbid in their import, chaotic in construction; although they sometimes seem the product of a delirious mind, they present, if we scrutinize them, a clearly discernible pattern. Man, and in particular Russian man, is confronted with three alternatives: He may follow his blind instincts (his "insect appetites") or the cold precepts of reason without love (the "Euclidian mind" of Ivan Karamazov) or the path of Christian love and joy (the way of Aliesha, the younger Karamazov). The third alternative, which leads to the liberation of man through Christ, is described in *The Brothers Karamazov*:

The vault of heaven full of soft, shining stars, stretched vast and fathomless. . . . The milky way ran in two pale streams from the zenith to the horizon. The fresh, motionless, still night enfolded the earth. The white towers and golden dome of the cathedral gleamed out against the sapphire sky. The gorgeous autumn flowers, in the beds around the house, were slumbering till morning. The silence on earth seemed to melt into the silence of the night. The mystery of earth was one with the mystery of the stars. . . . Aliesha stood, gazed and suddenly threw himself down on the earth. . . . He kissed it weeping, sobbing, watering it with his tears, and vowed passionately to love it for ever and ever:

"Water the earth with the tears of your joy, love those stars!"
echoed in his soul.[6]

The words of Staretz Zossima are reiterated in Aliesha's
consciousness:

My friends, pray God for gladness. Be glad as children, as the
birds of heaven. There is only one means of salvation, then take
yourself and make yourself responsible for all men's sins. . . . As
soon as you make yourself sincerely responsible for everything
and for all men, you will see at once that it is really so and that
you are to blame for everyone and for all things.[7]

From Zossima, the *pater seraphicus*, Aliesha has learned the
great lesson:

Love a man even in his sin, for that is the semblance of Divine
Love and is the highest love on earth. Love all God's creation, the
whole and every grain of sand in it. Love every leaf, every ray of
God's light. Love the animals, love the plants, love everything. If
you love everything, you will perceive the divine mystery of
things.[8]

This human solidarity in sin and retribution, this all-
embracing love is the burning core of Dostoievsky's world.
And even those of his heroes who have not received the rays of
God's light into their hearts are deeply aware of the necessity
for this solidarity. Thus in the famous dialogue between Aliesha
and Ivan Karamazov, it is Ivan the sceptic, the Euclidian
mind, who puts the question, Can the world's happiness be
built at the price of suffering? And he answers, that if human
happiness must be bought at the price of one tear of a little
child, we must reject it.

Dostoievsky wrote as a man transported out of his mind;
the rays of a supernatural world pervade his entire work. He

[6] *The Brothers Karamazov*, p. 380.
[7] *Ibid.*, p. 27.   [8] *Loc. cit.*

was more of a visionary than an artist, a mystic, not a moralist. Tolstoy, on the other hand, was the moralist and the consummate artist, the greatest that Russia has ever produced. Yet he put the effort to reach moral perfection, the quest of God, before his artistic endeavor. His personality is the product of the kenotic spirit inasmuch as he ardently desired to divest himself of all wealth, both material and cultural, in order to attain poverty. "Only when I shall have *nothing at all*," he said, "shall I be in a position to do some good."

Tolstoy's life has been closely scrutinized by biographers. We know his struggles: against himself, when he strove to overcome his passions; against his family and his surroundings when they became an obstacle to the simple life he wanted to lead. We know the storms of his dissipated youth, the remorse of his maturer years, and the tragedy of his old age; we remember that he fled from home and died in a little railroad station which, for a few days, became the dramatic center of Russia's life. And for the very reason that we know all this, because we have been allowed to read the various diaries, confessions, memoirs, and recollections written by Tolstoy himself and by the members of his family and his household, our vision of him is dimmed; or more correctly, he lives in our minds and not in our hearts.

Two conventional pictures have been painted of the "prophet of Yasnaia Poliana": one by his admirers, the other by his enemies. His admirers have represented him as a great sage who had renounced the vanities of the world and lived in a *thebaide*; who knew the answer to all questions, had discovered the path leading directly to absolute truth, and held the key to all wisdom. All religious, social, political, and ethical problems had been solved or were being solved by Tolstoy. Tolstoyanism was indeed a new creed, a new moral code in the making. His disciples often misunderstood him, distorted his teaching, interfered with his intimate life, and probably did him as much harm as his family. Tolstoy, who, in the years of his greatest sobriety, had retained a keen sense of humor, said that what he resented most were the Tolstoyans.

His enemies and critics, unable to subtract from his greatness as a writer, have pointed to the weakness of the man. They seek to show that he failed to live up to his ideals, that under his rough peasant blouse his flesh was as refined as when he was a young man-about-town in Moscow. They contend that he never had the courage to do away with everything; that while preaching the arduous life which the Raskolniki actually practiced, he lived in luxury; that when he became a vegetarian by conviction, the "Count's whim" required the expenditure of more money and of more care in the preparation of food than if he had been satisfied with ordinary fare. This man who was considered a saint abroad is described as a tyrant at home: He demanded endless sacrifices from his wife, made her bear thirteen children and copy out the manuscript of *War and Peace* seven times. For such devotion he showed no gratitude, but drove her nearly out of her mind by his fancies and exigencies. Finally, he left his family without a penny, having turned over all his author's rights to the public.

The true Tolstoy is, of course, presented in neither of these pictures. First of all, his role as a creative artist is too often forgotten both by the friends and by the enemies. Artists are said to be made of finer, more sensitive stuff than ordinary men. And Tolstoy was an artist, made of that subtler stuff which vibrated to the beauty of the world even when he had renounced its vanities. He was an extraordinary craftsman who worked for years on his novels. His drafts, rough copies, and notebooks, which have been recently published in the Soviet edition of his complete works, evidence the minute, patient, stubborn labor of Tolstoy. Among these posthumous works we find a number of variations of certain chapters which he rewrote completely, and even several times, before he was satisfied. These variations are as perfect, as carefully composed, as the final text. When asked why he cut out so much of what he had originally written, he would answer: "The stuff was good; there was nothing wrong with it; but it did not fit in with the rest. It was out of drawing. It had to be suppressed."

Little has been said about Tolstoy's culture. Because his moral teaching placed the people's wisdom above the learning of the upper classes, he has too often been considered an advocate of the uncultured mind. A Soviet learned society has recently compiled a descriptive catalogue of the French books in Tolstoy's library. It gives clear evidence of the extent of his reading, the intensity of his research, the breadth of his knowledge. And French literature was only one of the many branches he studied. Before he wrote *Resurrection* he read all the books devoted by famous French scientists to the social, legal, and medical aspects of prostitution. In preparation for *War and Peace*, he scrutinized every line written by Napoleon, jotting down notes on the margins of the books, using for his creative production a solid, well probed historical framework.[9]

His *Circle of Reading* is a four-volume collection of quotations, famous proverbs, thoughts, reflections borrowed for every day of the year from the great men, religious thinkers, and sages of all times and nationalities. This alone is an index to Tolstoy's culture. He studied Hebrew especially to read the Old Testament; he was well aware of the currents of Russian mysticism; he loved Pascal.

If we consider all this, we shall realize that it was not an easy task for this man to live the simple life. These treasures of culture, these subtle intellectual pleasures of an artist and a craftsman, were surely more difficult to renounce than the "luxury" of his home. The luxury of Tolstoy's home has, as a matter of fact, been very much exaggerated. He lived, like most Russian country gentlemen, in comfortable, homely surroundings, but Yasnaia Poliana was not a palatial mansion like the

[9] An excellent account of Tolstoy's collection of French books and his correspondence with French writers is contained in "Literaturnoye Nasledstvo": *Lev Tolstoy i Franzia.*

abodes of the Western aristocracy. Tolstoy himself was constant in his denunciation of the unrighteous possession of wealth; in fact he went so far as to consider it sinful to enjoy property. He was haunted by the idea that the refined life of the few was an evil example held up to the masses, corrupting them more surely than debauchery and drunken orgies.

It does not, after all, seem important whether Tolstoy lived up to his ideal of poverty in every detail of his life. The petty minds want to know whether he wore a silk shirt under his peasant blouse, whether his vegetarian meals were served on silver, and whether the boots he learned to make would really fit. By putting these questions, they clearly indicate that they miss the point. What Tolstoy achieved was real enough. He became aware that it was wrong to live complacently; to relish the fruits of culture while millions lived in ignorance; to be well fed and warmly clothed without giving a thought to the poor. He believed that a man should be able not only to create refined works of art but also to plough and reap as St. Theodosius and St. Sergius had taught long ago. And in this he is in harmony with the traditions of his people. In Russia's oldest cycles of legends, it is the little peasant Mikula Selianinovitch who is the greatest hero; it is Ivan the Fool who marries the tsar's daughter.

Tolstoy became keenly sensible of the fact that it is wrong to exercise violence, to persecute a helpless people. To Tsar Alexander III he wrote a famous letter denouncing capital punishment. He taught that one should not torment man or torture animals. And because he ran counter to the traditions of power, he lived in what the writer Merejkovsky describes as "a great and terrible solitude" of spirit.

For a decade and more, Yasnaia Poliana was a *thebaide* to which great men from all over Europe came to honour the Staretz in his rough white blouse. The people, too, understood him. A survey was recently made to find out whether, and to what extent, the masses remembered him. It was ascertained that there is a legend about him among the people. He is still spoken of as the man who gave up his riches, his comfort, his titles of nobility; who shared the life of the people, their sufferings and hopes. In their eyes he *did* live up to his ideals, and no doubt it is their appreciation which he would have placed above all others.

We have said that Tolstoy was not a mystic but a moralist. His novels show an extraordinary, almost uncanny gift of psychological analysis and introspection, but it may be said that he did not have a sense of the supernatural. Its rays did not penetrate his heart. This was his tragedy. His struggle against the church was a consequence of the fact that he was unaware of the Mystical Body. The sacramental life was a closed book to him. Christianity, in his eyes, was a moral teaching, not a revelation. Although he was deeply attached to the Gospels and applied himself to living in strict accord with their commandments, he did not grasp their essential teaching: that without the life of grace, it is impossible to achieve perfection.

Had Tolstoy lived in another age, his development might have been very different. He encountered religion in its most static, reactionary forms, enforced by the Russian state church and its debilitated hierarchy. He had the stuff of a great ascetic as he had the stuff of a great artist, but he misused it. His conscience was tragically torn. In order to understand his torment, it is only necessary to glance at his diaries, especially those of his later years, and at the dramatic confessions he wrote in 1910, a few months before his death. His pitiless self-criticism, his ardent desire of perfection, his efforts to attain to perfect love and meekness, his struggles against himself—all this is surprising in a man of his advanced age. It seemed that as the years passed his intellect sharpened, probing ever more deeply after his own sins and frailties.

Such a man could have been a saint had he known the truth wholly instead of in part. He would have realized that love and simplicity, meekness, nonresistence—all that he so passionately desired to achieve—are the free gifts of the God-man; that the redemption of man, however high his aims, must be the work of grace. Perhaps he had this intuition when, on his last journey, he knocked at the gates of the Shamardino convent. This man who had so bitterly attacked Orthodoxy, who appeared to have broken away from all the traditions of the Russian church, seemed now to be drawn by the white flame to become a wanderer in Christ.

XIV

The Prophet of Universality

ONE EVENING in the year 1875 a caravan of Bedouins who were wending their way across the African desert a few miles from Cairo caught sight of the solitary figure of a man clad in a dark frock coat and wearing a tall hat. The Bedouins stared in astonishment at this stranger, whose dress could scarcely have been less suitable. As the caravan vanished into the dusk, the man lay down on the sand and fell asleep. With the first rays of the sun he arose, shivering with cold. As he watched the dawn break, his pale face was illumined with joy. Slowly, he regained consciousness of his surroundings, turned back whence he had come, found the guides who were awaiting him at a distance, and drove to his Cairo hotel, to discover that his luggage was missing and that the Bedouins of the desert must have stolen his watch while he slept.

This incident, which is described by Wladimir Soloviev in one of his poems,[1] is autobiographical, and although the poet has a keen eye for the absurdity of his own appearance, the experience, in its interior aspect, was a milestone in his spiritual development. He had attained what he sought. In that moment of exaltation at dawn he had felt reflected within himself the vision of Sophia, God's Wisdom, the "unity of the world."

It is not usual to begin a study of Soloviev's life and work with this adventure in the Egyptian desert. Generally, his biographers start out with an enumeration of his scholarly

[1] *Tri Svidania.*

attainments: doctor of the Moscow university and of the divine academy; author of a thesis *The Crisis of Western Philosophy*; professor at the Woman's Higher School in Moscow. Even at this time (in his thirty-third year) he was an extremely learned man, well versed in physics, philology, history, theology, and the writings of the Eastern Fathers. Yet suddenly he had broken away from his scholarly pursuits and gone to London where, as he was engaged in the examination of ancient manuscripts at the British Museum, a mysterious inner voice had urged him to go to Egypt.

The poet Alexander Block, who was influenced by Soloviev's mysticism, justly stated that it was not Soloviev's scholarly research, but rather the vision beheld in the golden radiance of that African dawn, which was the key to his spiritual insight.[2] Like many youths of his time, Wladimir Soloviev had gone through a period of complete atheism. When he was fourteen he tore the ikons from the walls of his room. His contemporaries say that there was an element of fury in his godlessness. This period of atheism was succeeded by a stage in which he read Schopenhauer, Spinoza, and Kant, supplanting materialism by metaphysics. One day as he was traveling in a public coach, he tripped and almost fell out. A woman passenger caught him up, thus averting a fatal accident. At that very moment, in a flash, faith flowed into his soul. And with faith there was restored in his memory a vision of early childhood: a golden light, an interior image of indescribable loveliness. In his maturity he called it the world soul, God's Wisdom. It was this vision which he sought and re-experienced in Egypt, and shortly before his death he was to see it once again.

Soloviev began his philosophic career under the influence of the Slavophiles, by the aid of whose teachings he was able to discern the defects which lay at the root of the Orthodox Church's growing sterility. Guided by their principles, he developed and integrated his philosophical system. It has been

[2] Block, *Vladimir Soloviev i nashi Dni.*

said that he "cut through Orthodox official theology like an ice-breaker." At the same time, he pierced the materialistic creed of Moscow's intelligentsia with incisive logic. He was the first man who spoke of God in the university auditorium and provoked enthusiastic response.

Soloviev was an intimate friend of Dostoievsky. They mutually influenced each other during their seemingly interminable conversations, which are reflected in the dialogues of *The Brothers Karamazov*. From Dostoievsky Soloviev derived his idealistic concept of the Russian people as the "God-bearers," united with Christ in mystical love.

The nationalism of the Slavophiles informed much of Soloviev's early work, but when he became acquainted with *The Philosophical Letters* of Chaadaiev, which he discovered in Father Gagarin's French edition, his mental horizon widened to embrace a universal scheme. Although he preserved his belief in the mission of the Russian people, he now conceived the end of this mission as *unity*. Soloviev went deeper than the Slavophiles. He penetrated to the roots of the whole religious question, which is concerned not with the destiny of a nation but with the destiny of man. Thus there are two periods in Wladimir Soloviev's life and work. The period when he thought and wrote as an Orthodox theologian and the period during which his orientation was towards the Catholic Church. The most remarkable of the works belonging to the Orthodox period is *The Teaching of God-Humanity*.

Let us now look at Soloviev as he appeared to his contemporaries. He is described as "slim, dark, shut up in himself and somewhat enigmatic," as "exceedingly thin, almost emaciated," with a mane of dark hair, and eyebrows as black as charcoal, in striking contrast to the almost translucent pallor of his face. His blue-grey eyes were full of "mysterious beauty and sadness." [3] It is an unforgettable face, the face of a dreamer and a prophet. He was austere, often melancholy. (On the eve

[3] Motchulsky, *Wladimir Soloviev.*

of his sudden conversion, he had been, as he himself relates, "well-nigh to despair.") But he was subject to outbursts of almost wild gaiety; his laughter would ring out in a solemn assembly when least anticipated. It was in one of these light moods that he wrote of his journey to Egypt in comic verse, describing the frock coat, the tall hat, the lost luggage, and the inconveniences of a night in the desert.

Some of Soloviev's serious poems are of a vast religious inspiration, unfolding visions of majestic beauty; others are strange and eery as dreams. He was prolific, a brilliant journalist, a distinguished historian. His public speeches were intensely moving. In one of them he protested, like Tolstoy, against capital punishment, provoking a storm of enthusiasm from sympathizers and a storm of indignation from opponents. He was hailed as a true humanitarian by the intelligentsia, but the government compelled him to resign from the university faculty.

The political atmosphere was tense at that time. The serfs had been liberated in 1861, but the reform had come too late; it was unsatisfactory inasmuch as the emancipated peasants, who had not been provided with land, retained the feeling that they were the victims of injustice. The revolutionary movement was gathering force. Hundreds of young men and women were then "going to the people," which meant giving up their city careers and settling down in remote villages as teachers, doctors, and relief workers, sharing the arduous life of the masses whom they served. These young people preached socialism, and although the peasants were still too ignorant to absorb such teachings, the masses of the cities stirred with unrest and the accumulating forces of rebellion.

The young intelligentsia formed extremist currents. The "People's Will" movement was activated by a radical populism the principles of which were subsequently set forth by the Socialist-Revolutionary Party. These currents were not Marxist but traced their origins to the authentic Russian ideals of

WLADIMIR SOLOVIEV

ALEXANDER BLOCK——PORTRAIT BY K. SOMOV

social justice. Contrary to Marxism, which considers that the leading role must belong to the proletariat, that is, to the city working class, the revolutionary populists saw the true factor of social upheaval in the peasantry.

Radical populism applied terroristic methods. In 1882 Tsar Alexander II, the liberator of the serfs, was assassinated. The revolutionaries who committed this crime were arrested, tried, and condemned to death. It was on this occasion that both Soloviev and Tolstoy protested against capital punishment.

It is interesting to observe that the terrorist activities in Russia at that time were animated by a sacrificial motive. The young men involved considered the violences they committed as sins, but inevitable sins since Russia's transformation could not be effected by other methods. These sins of violence had to be expiated: the terrorists were prepared to die in atonement, and often they rejected the pardon offered them. The most striking example of this phenomenon is the instance of Ivan Kaliaev, the assassin of Grand Duke Sergius. Condemned to death, he declared in the courtroom that he believed in the teaching of Christ and was ready to give up his life for his brethren.

After Soloviev's famous speech against capital punishment, a new impetus was given to the discussion in Moscow's cultural circles of all these problems of populism, socialism, political violence, and the struggle for man's autonomy. In these controversies, Tolstoy's doctrine of nonresistance to evil was exposed as irrational by persons of a rationalistic temper and ardently espoused by persons of a religious temper. Militant atheism and mystical social aspirations were strangely blended in this society which had its source of unity in the necessity of protest.

Darwinism was eagerly absorbed by the student youth, who believed that science could give an answer to all questions. Soloviev parodied their teachings: "Man descends from the ape; therefore we must love each other!"

Looking about, Soloviev sought in vain an ideological foundation on which true humanism could be built. The aspirations of the Russian intelligentsia were lofty and generous; they led to heroism and self-sacrifice, but their very ardor was precipitous, since it lacked the sober spirituality essential to the middle way taught by the early mystics. During the course of many years he discussed these problems with Tolstoy. Yet he did not subscribe to Tolstoy's theory of nonresistance to evil. In fact he wrote a number of essays against it. Nor could he be satisfied with Slavophilism, which had degenerated, as we have observed, into a narrowly reactionary and nationalistic movement. Although conscious of Russia's national genius, he detested nationalistic complacency. He revealed himself as one of the first modern objectors to the doctrine of racial superiority when he spoke of "zoological nationalism." [4] He was also one of the first writers who openly undertook the defense of the Jews in Russia. "The Jewish problem," he declared, "is a Christian problem. We have not learnt to treat the Jews according to Christian principles. . . . We are separated from the Jews because we are not completely Christian." [5]

Zoological nationalism, terrorism, scientism, nonresistance, the mediocre teachings of the official church—none of these could satisfy Soloviev. In his famous speech against capital punishment he had said that he believed in the absolute value of the human person because he believed in Christ. "Nature tends towards absolute unity; human nature and the external world have the same soul, and this soul seeks to give birth to a divinity." In these words he summed up the doctrine which he had fully developed in *The Teaching of God-Humanity*.

Soloviev's works presaged the dawn of our twentieth century

[4] *The National Problem and Russia.*

[5] *Judaism and the Christian Problem.* He was supported by Tolstoy, who wrote to him: "If you express your thoughts on that subject, I know in advance that you will also express my feelings and thoughts, because the foundation of our repulsion towards the persecution of Jewish nationality is the same: the feeling of a brotherly bond with all peoples, especially with the Jews, among whom Christ was born." (March 15, 1890)

Christian humanism. One of his most distinctive achievements is that he set forth in works of strength and clarity the doctrine of the divine origin of man. He placed the God-man at the center of creation and showed the whole world to be informed by the Trinitarian principle. The incarnation of the Word took place in the Person of Jesus Christ, but there is an incarnation of God in each man, created in His image. Each person is a "man-God," a member of the Mystical Body. God is also incarnated in Christian society, reflecting Divine justice. Social ethics must be rooted in the Divinity.

Soloviev describes God as an absolute and perfect *whole*. The world is the expression of Divine thought and love. There is a fullness, a *totality of being*: the plurality of created things is merged in a supreme unity. The unity of the world is its soul. Soloviev also calls it God's Wisdom (Sophia in Greek) which is described in the Book of Proverbs.

The Lord possessed me in the beginning of his ways, before he made anything from the beginning. . . . I was with him forming all things: and was delighted every day, playing before him at all times; Playing in the world. And my delights *were* to be with the children of men. (8, 22–31)

It is this vision of Sophia which haunted Soloviev from his early childhood and appeared to him in the Egyptian desert. The principle of unity was disclosed to him with extraordinary clarity. Whatever the intricacy of his metaphysical dreams, this absolute totality of things is the flaming center of his teaching. "Apart from God," he wrote, "Who is the very principle of Unity, no union is possible." He expressed this total harmony in one of his most beautiful poems:

> The barriers fall, the chains are smelted
> By Divine fire,
> And the eternal morning of new life
> Rises in all, and all in one.

Soloviev's christological interpretation of the world led him towards ethical principles which he described in his famous work *The Justification of Good*. It is the basis of his social teaching, which was carried on by his disciple Nicholas Berdiaev and has continued to stimulate modern Orthodox thought. It coincides with Western Catholic trends, with the Christian humanism of Jacques Maritain. Soloviev may be considered the precursor of personalism.

As he turned from nationalist Orthodoxy and towards a universal scheme, the world's unity in Christ, Soloviev evolved what he called his theocratic teaching. In his scheme of absolute totality, humanity was to be ruled by a theocracy founded on three fundamental principals: the high priest (Rome); the king (Byzantium); the prophet (Russia). At the end of his life, he gave up these somewhat artificial constructions, ceasing to believe that it was possible for God's wisdom to be fully expressed in a society on earth. But he retained the idea of a world whose various streams were irresistibly flowing towards unity. In one of his last works, *The Three Conversations,* he describes the union of the churches taking place at the end of the world as the culmination of a struggle against the Antichrist. The conversion of the Jews was also part of the ultimate fulfilment. So deep was his concern for them that during his last illness he asked his friends to wake him if he fell asleep, since he had to pray for the Jews.

It is in this revelation of unity that we must seek the key to Soloviev's Catholicism. It is usual to stress his historical studies and his criticism of the Russian Orthodox Church and of static Byzantium as the source of his Catholic sympathies. True, he did uncover the failings of Byzantine and Russian Orthodoxy resulting from their dependence on the secular power. He deplored the inactivity of the Orthodox Church, its fear (like that of St. Cassien in the legend) of soiling its robes. But what he said about these failings was an echo of Slavophile thought, the bitter criticisms of which he hardly exceeded. He was not a spiritual émigré but was deeply attached to Russian culture. Like Chaadaiev, but much more forcibly, he spoke of the mission of the Russian people and predicted its fulfilment.

What Soloviev felt most acutely was the break in Christian unity which had resulted from the Great Schism. The Orthodox Church was a limb severed from the Universal Church, and this was the cause of its weakness. Therefore, he conceived the reunion of the churches as an organic process like the healing of a wound, a supernatural fusion of the two great members of the Mystical Body. He liked to reiterate that this reunion, this fusion, "must not be mechanical, but chemical," and he would add, "An inner voice whispers to me: study chemistry, study chemistry . . . At first, I thought that I was actually to study the chemical sciences; later I understood what it all meant."

Like Yury Krijanitch two hundred years earlier, Soloviev looked upon the Russians not as schismatics but as separated brothers. He recognized "the eminently religious character of the Russian people and the mystical tendency manifested in our philosophy, in art and in literature." [6] He advocated the faithful observance of the Eastern rite, fervently supporting the Slavonic liturgist and apostle of union, Bishop Strossmayer of Bosnia and Sirmium, whom he visited at Zagreb. In the various essays which he devoted to the subject of union, and especially in his works *The Russian Idea* and *Russia and the Universal Church*, Soloviev very clearly stated that when a Russian joins Rome it is not an instance of abjuration (as in the case of conversion from Protestantism) but of reunion, a simple return to the common fold from which the Orthodox was separated by historical circumstance.

Here also he follows in the wake of Krijanitch, and we know that the Vatican of today has adopted the same point of view.

[6] *La Russie et l'Église Universelle.* This essay was written in French and published in Paris, because of the difficulties of censorship which Soloviev would have incurred in Russia. It was later translated into Russian and is included in his complete works published in St. Petersburg.

The Holy See recommends that all Russians joining the Catholic Church shall remain in their own rite and in their native milieu instead of being latinized and denationalized as were the nineteenth-century Russian Catholics. These recommendations have been clearly set forth in the Encyclical *Orientalium Dignitas*, and no Russian can ignore them.

Soloviev's most complete profession of faith concerning the question of union is to be found in his *nota bene* at the end of *Russia and the Universal Church*:

As a member of the true and venerable Orthodox Eastern or Greek Eastern Church, which speaks not through an anti-canonical Synod, nor through the officials of secular power, but through the voice of its great Fathers and Doctors, I recognize as supreme judge in matters of religion him who has been recognized as such by Saint Ireneus, Saint Denis the Great, Saint Athanasius the Great, Saint John Chrysostom, Saint Cyrill, Saint Flavian, the Blessed Theodat, Saint Maxim the Confessor, Saint Theodore the Studite, Saint Ignacius, etc.—that is the Apostle Peter who lives in his successors and who has not heard in vain the words of the Lord: "Thou art Peter, and upon this rock I shall build My Church. Confirm thy brethren. Feed My sheep, feed My lambs." Immortal spirit of the blessed apostle, invisible minister of the Lord in the government of His visible Church, you know that it needs an earthly body to manifest itself. Twice already thou hast given it a social body: first, in the Greco-Roman world and then in the Romano-German world; thou hast placed under its sway the Empire of Constantine and the Empire of Charlemagne. After these two temporary incarnations, it awaits its third and last incarnation. A whole world of strength and desire, but without a clear consciousness of its destiny, knocks at the door of universal history. What is your word, people of the word? Your masses do not know it as yet, but powerful voices arising from your midst have already revealed it. Two centuries ago, a Croat priest announced it prophetically, and in our days, a Bishop belonging to the same nation has proclaimed it many times with admirable eloquence. That which has been said by the representatives of the Western Slavs, the great Krijanitch and the great Strossmayer, needed but a simple *amen* from the Eastern Slavs. I come to say this *amen* in the name of a hundred million Russian Christians, trusting fully and firmly that they will not disavow me.[7]

Thus the great mission of the Russian people, their as yet "unspoken word," as Dostoievsky called it, was to achieve unity. This is "the Russian idea" of Soloviev. Like the author of *The Brothers Karamazov*, he saw Russia moving towards universality (although along a different path).

There has long been much discussion in Russia as to whether Soloviev actually joined the Catholic Church. Although the issue remains controversial, we have the testimony of Father Nicholas Tolstoy, a Catholic priest of the Eastern rite, that he himself received Soloviev's adhesion. According to this account Soloviev was received into the Church of Rome on February 18, 1896 in Father Tolstoy's private chapel in Moscow. The documents in connection with the ceremony were signed by the priest and two witnesses, Princess Olga Dolgoruky and Dmitry Novsky.[8] Soloviev's reception into the church is thought to have been kept in complete secrecy because of the restrictions on religious freedom then existing in Russia. Conflicting inferences are drawn from the circumstances of Soloviev's death. Taken ill in the country home of one of his friends, he called for an Orthodox priest, who administered the last sacraments. The Orthodox present the record of this last act of his life as proof that he had returned to the mother church (or had never left it). The Catholics argue that there being no Catholic priest at hand, he was permitted and even advised by his religion to receive Holy Communion *in extremis* from the hands of an Orthodox priest. To fetch a Catholic priest from Moscow might have been materially impossible; or at least, the priest in

[7] *Ibid.*

[8] This testimony was published in the Russian Catholic review *Kitej*, in Warsaw (No. 8, December 12, 1927). Father Tolstoy also published a letter describing the circumstances of the event in the Paris review *Univers*, September 9, 1910.

question would have been exposed to danger, since his movements would have been followed by the police.

Soloviev is still claimed by both Orthodox and Catholics. And this may be providential inasmuch as he forms a spiritual bond between men otherwise divided. Even his grave is a symbol of that union of which he was the first Russian apostle: pious hands have placed side by side an Orthodox ikon representing the Resurrection and the image of Our Lady of Ostrobram, devotion to whom is spread among Catholics of Eastern rite.

Shortly before his death, Soloviev said, wearily, "The works of God are difficult." Indeed he was an unflagging worker in God's fields, and when he passed away he could not see how fertile his labors had been; he could see only the difficulty. Actually, his influence has been immense among his people. His thought has been the source of three main intellectual and spiritual currents, each of which has continued to be at work in Russian culture.

To the Orthodox he left the inspiration of his teaching concerning the God-humanity, which broke down the frozen walls of official theology. A new school of religious thought sprang up in Orthodox circles, which produced a deep religious revival in Petersburg on the eve of the Revolution. His words inspired remarkable theologians and philosophers like Nicholas Berdiaev and Father Sergius Bulgakov. During the Revolution, the Russian Orthodox exiled abroad preserved this message; the Russian Divine Academy of Paris, which has done so much to nurture the white flame of Orthodoxy, based its teaching on the doctrine of the God-man.

Soloviev has also inspired the Russian school of symbolist poets headed by Alexander Block and Andrei Biely. Block, especially, reflects the mysticism of Soloviev's poems—his eery day dreams, his visions of God's Wisdom, garbed in gold and azure. And Block is considered Russia's greatest modern poet.

The third current created by Soloviev is the new Russian

Catholic movement which developed in Moscow during the years preceding the Revolution. For the first time, Russians who joined Rome remained rooted in their national soil, learning to treasure their own liturgy and their cultural traditions.[9] No longer was there the necessity of choosing between their country and their faith. Russian Catholics became members of the universal church without abandoning the venerable traditions of their fathers.

These three currents are merged in Soloviev's own profession of faith. Addressing himself to the Russian people, he concludes:

Your word, O people of the word, is free and universal theocracy, the true solidarity of all classes, Christianity practiced in public life, the Christianization of politics; it is the freedom of all the oppressed, the protection of all the weak; it is social justice and the good Christian peace.[10]

This is the message of Wladimir Soloviev, which can be shared by both Catholics and Orthodox. It is their common heritage of Christian humanism preserved throughout the centuries. It is the true Russian idea expressed by all great Russian spiritual leaders from St. Sergius to Dostoievsky.

[9] The ban on the practice of Catholicism was lifted in 1903.
[10] Soloviev, *op. cit.*

XV

The Twilight Men[1]

DURING THE YEARS preceding the revolution of 1917 Russia was steeped in an atmosphere of intense, almost mystical expectation. It seemed as if the storm gathering on the horizon were already oppressing the supersensitive minds of writers and thinkers.

"As a witness not wholly deprived of sight and hearing," wrote the poet Alexander Block, "I permit myself to point out that January 1901 was placed under quite another sign than December 1900; the very beginning of the century was filled with essentially new symbols and presentiments.[2] In the words of Andrei Biely, another gifted poet, it was an epoch of "glowing skies," of "twilight." Not only Block and Biely but that entire generation of young intellectuals perceived that the rays which were casting their light obliquely over Russia were those of sunset. Tchekhov's plays, especially *The Three Sisters*, were conceived in the stifling atmosphere which presaged the storm, and in the writings immediately preceding the revolutionary outbreak are reflected the first flashes of lightning, weirdly illuminating a doomed world.

It can be truly said that the Russian intelligentsia entered this tragic time with open eyes. Some welcomed the approaching cataclysm as an apocalypse; others tried desperately to avert it; still others strove to transfigure it by spiritual reinter-

[1] By courtesy of *The Review of Politics*, Notre Dame, Indiana, in the July 1943 issue of which this material originally appeared.
[2] Quoted by Biely in *Natchalo Vieka*.

pretation. This peculiar clairvoyance was purely intuitive, at times even prophetic. To quote Andrei Biely once more, these men were treading "the foothills," leading to the "crests" of revolution: they had entered the "zone of mists." "In 1914, we were caught in a mountain blizzard. . . . We shall not descend into the valley before the twenty-first century." [3]

Although the writers who moulded Russian thought during those years were influenced by political events, they did not think in political terms. They conceived the approaching catastrophe as an acute religious crisis in which the souls of men would be shaken, perhaps shattered. But this experience would finally lead Russia, perhaps the entire world, towards a spiritual rebirth.

Dostoievsky had said that Pushkin left "an unspoken word." Dostoievsky himself remained an unspoken word, a mystery to the core of which those who followed him sought to penetrate. Most writers of that time composed variations on the Dostoievsky theme. This tendency distinguishes them from the Soviet literary school, which is entirely devoid of his influence. The comments, essays, and meditations concerning the author of *The Brothers Karamazov*, of which the works of Merejkovsky and Vassily Rozanov are typical, present certain distortions, not because they lack profundity or brilliance but because they are marked with an extreme sophistication, a kind of intellectual pride, which is entirely alien to the great novelist. When Merejkovsky wrote his *Antichrist* or when he spoke of the advent of the "Kingdom of the Spirit," he was actually contemplating a new religion which he called the "Third Testament," an "eschatological Christianity." It was hailed by radical religious groups as a coming "Russian reformation." The idea of reformation had certainly never entered Dostoievsky's mind. These religious speculations reveal the extreme tension of those days, when all values were being not

[3] Biely, "Eupopeia," editorial in No. 1 of the review *Epopeia,* Moscow-Berlin, 1922.

only revised but melted and recast in the flames of a new apocalypse.

In 1903 Merejkovsky, his wife, Zinaida Hippius (a highly gifted poetess of the symbolist school), and a number of their friends became the leaders of the "religious-philosophical movement," which was to play an important part in Russia's spiritual revival. They found the review *Novy Put* ("New Path") which published the works of outstanding thinkers, writers, and poets. Among the other sponsors of the movement were Nicholas Berdiaev, who was to become an internationally known religious thinker, and Serge Bulgakov, a brilliant young economist who entered the priesthood and is now considered one of the most distinguished of Russian theologians. And there was Paul Florensky, a sober scientist and mathematician, who also became a priest and wrote *The Pillar and Foundation of Truth*, a book which has exercised a profound influence on modern Orthodox thought.

This group organized meetings and debates which brought together the élite of the Orthodox clergy and the religious-minded intelligentsia. This meeting of the clerical and lay mind was something new in Russian cultural life. During the preceding decades the leaders of the intelligentsia had been for the most part inspired by Western atheism and determinism. Those who had followed spiritual trends had formed a minority who evolved their ideology outside the official Church (like Tolstoy) or became solitary thinkers (like Soloviev). Even Dostoievsky, whose thinking was so deeply imbued with Orthodoxy, had failed to achieve a reconciliation between the intellectuals and the official church.

Religious revival was given a further impulse by the publication of *Vekhi* ("Landmarks"). This was a collection of essays pointing to the necessity of reestablishing the primacy of the spirit in individual lives as well as in the political and social realms. The first attempt to combat materialism at its very root and to replace it by a world concept based on religion, it stressed the supreme dignity of the human person and was, so to speak, the first "personalist manifesto" of the age. Berdiaev, Bulgakov, and another young professor, Peter Struve, all three of whom contributed to *Vekhi*, were former Marxists who had supplanted historical materialism by Christian idealism, and this fact gave a particular value to their testimony, since it proved that men scientifically trained were no longer satisfied with atheist socialism; their very contribution to such a work evidenced the fact that social justice was not necessarily linked with a godless doctrine. In a famous essay Berdiaev reproached the intelligentsia for having replaced philosophy with "utilitarian" political standards, of having ignored the messages of Tolstoy and Soloviev.

Thus on the eve of Lenin's godless onslaught Russian culture was resolutely turning towards spirituality. Orthodoxy, which until then had found support largely in reactionary groups, now penetrated into liberal and socialist circles, in which there developed a radical messianism inspired by Russia's highest religious and social ideals.

Lenin, the Bolshevist leader, was greatly irritated and disturbed by the publication of *Vekhi*. He accused its contributors of being the exponents of "Russian reactionary bourgeois liberalism." So bitter was his indictment that Biely wrote that the Bolshevists leader had dealt with *Vekhi* through court martial.

Standing alone among the various groups striving to revise Russian cultural, social, and religious values was Vassily Rozanov, a powerful and original thinker. The son of a poor middle class family, he spent most of his life in small provincial towns, where he taught history and geography in secondary schools; when he later served as a minor official in Petersburg, he was still very poor.

Rozanov married Appollinaria Suslova, who in her youth had been Dostoievsky's companion and the cause of the great novelist's intimate tragedy. Her marriage with Rozanov, whom she left after three years, was no less unhappy, but in spite of bitter memories Rozanov admitted that this dramatic association had yielded him a deeper knowledge of Dostoievsky. He was a fervent admirer of the author of *The Brothers Karamazov*, and no Russian critic has had more profound insight into Dostoievsky's genius. One of Rozanov's most remarkable works is an essay on *The Grand Inquisitor*.

Rozanov was a contributor to *Novoie Vremia*, a daily newspaper which was the leading organ of Petersburg reactionaries; yet he cannot be described as a reactionary in the ordinary sense of the word. It is true that he was an antagonist of the liberal intelligentsia; he was in sympathy with extreme nationalistic views and had been expelled from the religious-philosophical group for his antisemitic writings. Judged by purely political standards, he was indeed a stark retrograde, but political standards can scarcely be applied to him. Rozanov's thought soared above programs and slogans. His pronouncements are paradoxical and often harsh in the extreme, but they are not partisan. Although in the beginning he advocated "pogroms" with revolting cynicism, he later requested that his antisemitic writings be destroyed. He even spoke in defense of Judaism as a genuinely organic religion, the religion of the "fruitful womb," to be evaluated above Christian asceticism. He was a firm believer in the authority, however intangible, of the Russian Orthodox Church; he denounced religious tolerance (his polemic directed against Soloviev was particularly bitter on that subject). Yet he himself was in rebellion against Christianity: some of his essays are strikingly nonconformist, even unorthodox.

Both in his likes and dislikes Rozanov was concerned least of all with the political and social aspects of the issue involved. He was absorbed in purely religious speculations to which he gave perfect form. He was a brilliant stylist, and although some of his writings are so crudely realistic as to be almost unfit for print, none of them are tainted with perversion or blasphemous in their import. Even when he revolted against Christ, he continued to be inexplicably drawn by His sweetness, which he feared more than His power. And he was aware of the Christian sources of Russia's culture: "Is not all of Russia in the Church?" he wrote. "Outside its walls what would remain?" [4]

Rozanov may be said to represent that anti-liberal school which sought to forestall the gathering storm through "ideological counter revolution." Alexander Block, on the other hand, was the exponent of that radical messianism which strove to interpret the cataclysm in spiritual terms. Block was the central figure of the symbolist group which comprises Fedor Sologub, Andrei Biely, Vyacheslav Ivanov, Valery Bryusov, Constantine Balmont and Zinaida Hippius—a brilliant pleiad of poetic geniuses surrounded by a swarm of minor talents. The Russian symbolists brought forth a remarkable poetical revival. Their rise was due to a variety of influences both in Russia and abroad. We can trace their inspiration to its wellsprings in French symbolist poetry, in the work of Edgar Allan Poe and Maeterlinck, and in the mysticism of Soloviev. Their ideology is linked to the thinking if Fichte, Schopenhauer, and Nietzsche and the anthroposophist teaching of Dr. Rudolf Steiner, the German thinker, who at that time had many followers in Russia. The works produced by the symbolist school are pieces of rare craftsmanship steeped in that mystical atmosphere of the twilight years.

Alexander Block belonged to the Russian intelligentsia, to all that was best and most essential in their culture. His father was professor of public law at the University of Warsaw; his mother was the daughter of an eminent scientist. He married the daughter of the world-famous chemist Mendeleiev and was intimate with Soloviev's family, especially with Soloviev's favorite nephew, the poet Serge Soloviev. He was not only a great man of letters but an outstanding personality. "All who

[4] Rozanov, *Opavshie Listia*.

knew him," writes Mirsky, "felt in him the presence of a
superior being. Very handsome, he was a splendid specimen of
what it has become fashionable to call the Nordic race [his
father came from an old Holstein family]. He was the meeting-
point of several lines of tradition—he was both very Russian
and very European." [5] Biely, his intimate friend and biographer, speaks of him as a "fairy-prince," a broad-shouldered,
athletic young man with "soft, ash-colored hair" and sun-
burned cheeks which seemed to reflect the glow of summer
skies. But this young Viking was a dreamer and a visionary.

As we have said, Block and all the other symbolists were
strongly influenced by the mystical poetry of Wladimir Soloviev. For them, God's Wisdom, Sophia, became indeed a living
reality. She filled the glowing skies of their youth and pervaded
their imaginative life. So vivid was this mysterious presence
that on one occasion Serge Soloviev roamed all night through
the woods on the Blocks' estate in order to "meet the dawn,"
as Wladimar Soloviev met Sophia in the desert. His absence
caused so much anxiety and distress that Block and his wife
rebuked him when he returned. Very much surprised, he
answered that he could not disobey "the beautiful lady's call,"
and that they were all to share in the message he had brought
back.

This story is illustrative of the way in which these young
symbolists thought and felt. Like Soloviev they looked, half in
jest and half in earnest, for mysterious signs and revelations.
They lived in a day dream, in what Mirsky calls a mystical
realism of extraordinary intensity.

Block's early poems are inspired by Wladimir Soloviev's
theme. The world of his first youth is one of dreamy sweetness,
aerial music, and love. The beautiful lady rides in gold and
azure skies or appears in the soft rays of summer sunsets. But
soon the scene changes. The horizon now glows not gold but
crimson. Night descends and the celestial lady is transformed

[5] Mirsky, *Contemporary Russian Literature,* p. 211.

into a prostitute, the captivating stranger of the poem which
made Block famous:

> And every evening at the appointed hour
> (Or is it only a dream of mine?)
> A maidenly figure, caught in tight silks,
> Moves in the hazy window.[6]

From that time on, between 1905 and 1914, Block's bright
vision was obscured by wine, passion, women, and the smoke
of taverns and suburban cabarets haunted by the stranger. The
wild nights, the Gypsy songs, the eery silence of sombre, snow-
clad back streets, re-echo in his poems. And then the stranger
undergoes another transformation. She is neither the gentle
vision of his youth nor the mysterious figure of the pleasure
haunts, but the incarnation of a new reality, purified, transfigured: the image of Russia, which now becomes the central
theme of Blocks' poetry. "Oh Russia, my wife!" he exclaims in
one of his poems, and it seemed indeed that he was wedded to
his native land by a mystical tie which revealed to him the very
depths of the people's soul.

Although he was acutely conscious of the tragic nature of
the approaching crisis, Block never became directly interested
in politics. He espoused no ideology. On a visit to the editorial
office of a review run by his friends, he declared: "This is not
for me! You are philosophers and political leaders and I am a
mystic!" On the margin of a book dealing with spiritual aridity
he wrote, "I know, I know it all!" As he himself declared with
great emphasis on several occasions, he heard "the music of the
time, the noise of the epoch." His gaze was fixed on the destinies of Russia. He saw her swiftly moving towards catastrophe
on a cosmic scale. Already he could perceive the poisonous
mists of the Bolshevist temptation rising over his native fields
and villages. He said that he did not know "how to pity Russia"
but bore "her cross carefully." He predicted that she would

[6] *Ibid.*, p. 214.

"give her wild beauty to a wizard" who would "entice and betray her." But she would never "lose herself," only "her fair brow" would be "clouded with sorrow." Beyond the tragedy he descried the true face of his country, the sorrowful features of what he called "beggar Russia," her humility and her inarticulate genius.

The Russian symbolists believed that they were endowed with second sight which enabled them to receive special revelations. Critics have found their work defective in its mannerisms, its excessive intricacy of thought and imagery. But although Block was born into this decadent age, he never indulged in such exaggerations. His inspiration is essentially classical. Even his obscurity, his darkest symbolism, makes sense. Looking back, we understand that his work was prophetic.

It was during this period that Block wrote *The Field of Kulikovo*, depicting the battle of the ancient Russian princes against the Mongols. In *The Field of Kulikovo* he attained not only to complete mastery of his poetic medium but to a deep comprehension of Russia's historical destinies. It is what Andrei Biely described as Block's flaming civic inspiration.

The mountain blizzard weighed heavily upon that generation of Russia's twilight years which lived to see the tragic dawn. But in spite of their intellectual and spiritual confusion, they watched with breathless interest the beginning of the new era. Certain fragments of their peculiar ideology even survived during the first years of Revolution.

In 1917 and 1918, national messianism was given a new impulse by Andrei Biely and Alexander Block. At that time these poets emerged from their aloofness and drew closer to political life. They were adherents of the extreme left Socialist-Revolutionary Party who, without sharing the aims and doctrines of communism, welcomed the revolution as the fulfilment of Russia's social mission. Eventually, this party was crushed by the rise of the Communists. But for such men as Block and Biely, the Revolution was above all the realization of their eschatological presentiments. It was the crucifixion of Russia, which was to lead to her resurrection. Speaking of her ordeal, Biely exclaims: "I know all, I know nothing, I love, I love, I love!" He pictures Russia nailed to the cross, yet full of mystical expectation:

> Russia—you are today the bride,
> Receive the message of Spring.[7]

Among the writings published in the early years of the Bolshevist régime, the dialogue between the symbolist poet and essayist Vyacheslav Ivanov and the critic Gershenson (a former contributor to *Vekhi*) merits consideration. While they both lay sick in a hospital, sharing the same ward, these men wrote each other letters discussing the destinies of culture which were later collected in a small volume entitled *Correspondence between Two Corners*. Vyacheslav Ivanov, the great classical scholar, wrote on behalf of the *thesaurus* in which the cultural values subject to the impact of revolution might be preserved: Gershenson, the critic, looked upon the prospect of the *tabula rasa* as a gain; he welcomed the revolutionary gale which was sweeping away a world weighed down with too much knowledge and too many intellectual habits.

Both authors were well acquainted with all the intricacies of philosophical and religious speculations. They couched their thoughts in an elaborate and brilliant style. It is indeed a remarkable dialogue, especially when we recall that these two men who represented the Russian intellectual élite were calmly discussing the problems of culture among the ruins of their shattered world.

In a letter to Charles du Bos written in 1930 [8] (when the poet escaped from Russia), Vyacheslav Ivanov explained that his desire to preserve the cultural heritage had been dictated by a consideration weightier than a mere intellectual appreciation

[7] *Christoss Voskresse.*
[8] Published in *Vigile*, No. 2, Paris, 1931.

of values. It had been the universal Christian culture of which he depored the loss. "Christianity," he wrote, "being absolute religion, has the power of reviving the ontological memory of civilization." In Christian tradition he perceived not a rigid, lifeless mould, an intolerable weight of knowledge, but an ever-creative source of rejuvenation. And it was to the universal church that Ivanov finally turned. In Rome, where he took refuge, he became a Catholic of the Eastern rite.

Not only Vyacheslav Ivanov and Gershenson but most writers and poets who had survived the revolutionary storm discussed this momentous question. Rozanov, Merejkovsky, Berdiaev, Bulgakov, and many others have devoted many pages to it. But it was Alexander Block who described most colorfully and most esoterically the riddle of the revolution in his poem *The Twelve*. He pictured twelve red soldiers marching through the streets in a snowstorm, a wild, reckless twelve, "ripe for death and daring, pitying none."

> The wind is a whirl, the snow is a dance
> In the night twelve men advance
> Black narrow rifle straps
> Cigarettes, tilted caps,
> A convict's stripes would fit their backs.[9]

The twelve men are plunderers and murderers. "At Holy Russia let's fire a shot!" they cry, and as their wild words ring out the starving mongrel which ambles after them (the Old World about to die) trembles with the cold.

These lines of the poet of the beautiful lady are characterized by the most sombre realism, the crudest cynicism. *The Twelve* is a *tchasstushka*, a factory workers' song, in which a weird harmony is wrought of the shrill notes of the harmonica, the howling of the blizzard, and the moans of the girl victim whom one of the soldiers has left for dead. Yet the poem culminates astonishingly in a vision, luminous and majestic.

[9] Translated by Abraham Yarmolinsky and Babette Deutsch.

Suddenly, "where the vagrant snow-veils veer," enveloped in the "snow of diamonds" Christ appears, carrying the red banner. Unharmed by the bullets, "in the mist-white roses garlanded, He marches on. And the twelve are led."

The poem awakened surprise, enthusiasm, indignation. Biely and his friends hailed it as the new apocalypse. But Zinaida Hippius, who had been among the first to recognize Block's genius, wrote bitterly:

> I shall not forgive. Your soul is innocent.
> I shall never forgive it.

Had Block, the mystic, the visionary, the purest poet of his time, profaned the sacred world he had disclosed? He did not answer this question but wrote, enigmatically:

> In January 1918, I abandoned myself for the last time to the elements. . . . I do not retract what I then wrote, because it was written in accordance with the elements: for instance, when I composed "The Twelve" and after I had finished the poem, I heard for several days with my physical ear a great noise around me—a confused noise, probably the noise of the crumbling world.[10]

Those who sought hasty conclusions accused the author of *The Twelve* of having become an adherent of the Bolshevist régime. But nothing in Block's attitude towards Russia's new masters can justify such an interpretation. He was not even their fellow-traveler. He kept aloof, a tragic and solitary figure, suffering as great privations as the others of his group. He died of exhaustion in 1921, two years after Rozanov. The Bolshevists never regarded him as their poet; they resented his prophetic utterances as they resented Biely's eschatology. It is only today, when the consciousness of nationality is being revived in Russia, that Block's reputation has been gradually reestab-

[10] Block, "Posthumous Diary." Quoted in Biely's *Vosspominania o Bloke.*

lished. And it is *The Field of Kulikovo* and not *The Twelve*
which is most often quoted in recent Soviet publications. That
he retained his integrity until the end is testified by Biely, who
wrote that although Block's heart "reflected Russia" and "beat
in unison with the future," he never bowed before false values.
He perished in the stifling atmosphere of communism "without
ever saying: 'Let it be.' " [11]

Block was not with this or that régime, he was with Russia
and her people. He beheld Christ leading his people to salvation in spite of the crimes of the few. Today the religious spirit
of the Russia he loved is reasserting itself, strengthened and
purified through suffering, and we are more able to apprehend
the meaning which the symbolism of *The Twelve* sought to
convey. Nevertheless the fact remains that Alexander Block and
the other men of this period of expectant dusk were inclined
towards paradox in thought and imagery. This polarity is sometimes disturbing. Their inspiration wandered through laby-
rinths full of strange echoes and shadows.

The flaw in their realism, from the Christian standpoint,
consists in the fact that they approached the christological
theme without an authentic consciousness of the person of
Christ. They did not know His humanity, His grace, His
wisdom. Thus He remains for them an apparition, not the
all-loving God-man. They were followers of Dostoievsky, but
none of them had Dostoievsky's mystical experience. And yet
these men of twilight held the outposts of spirituality against
the Bolshevist godless offensive. They were the last to be aware
that the children of men were destined for light and freedom
in the spirit. Not one of them said the fatal: "Let it be." Their
peculiar merit is that they bore witness to Christ and the spirit
in a world where Christ and the spirit were soon to be crucified.

[11] *Ibid.*

XVI

The Soul of Russia Today

AS THE READER looks back on a thousand years of Russian Christian and humanist tradition, he will realize why Lenin's godless myth could not triumph. True, the leaders of Russian Communism benefited by this tradition, at least in the beginning. It is apparent that Marxist collectivism could be presented as a form of society which would afford fulfilment to the people's social aspirations. The Russian ideology of the MIR, the concept of property as something to be acquired through work, the disapprobation in which the wealthy landlord and the Kulak were held—all these ideas had a superficial correspondence with communist doctrine. The Bolshevists skillfully built upon this ready-made foundation in inciting the people to rebellion.

On the eve of Lenin's rise to power the masses had participated in the first outbreak, the February Revolution of spring 1917, which effected the downfall of the monarchy and the institution of a true democratic régime. Preparation of a land-reform bill was then begun and plans were made for the summoning of a constituent assembly which would determine the form of Russia's new government. These measures were based on the program of the Socialist-Revolutionary Party, which, as we have seen, had its ideological foundation in the anti-totalitarian, non-Marxist populist tradition. It is important to stress the point that in the elections to the constituent assembly, which took place in the early fall of 1917, it was the populist group which gained the majority of votes, the bourgeois parties and the Bolshevists representing a minority.

Complete freedom of religion was proclaimed in Russia at that time. The patriarchate, suppressed by Peter the Great, was re-established and a patriarch elected, and a new impulse was given to religious life. Russia was swiftly moving towards that order inspired by her own ideals of social justice which her people, her great writers and thinkers, and her spiritual leaders, had evolved through the centuries. But she had been shaken by a long and exhausting war. The people were disturbed by a deep unrest characterized by confused feelings of rebellion, lassitude, and smouldering distrust. The new régime, which was obliged to wage war at the front while fighting anarchy at home, was unable to cope immediately with the innumerable problems created by the revolution. The atmosphere was filled with a growing impatience and doubt arising from the fear of the masses that the old order might be restored and their hostility towards the bourgeoisie who, although they had effected the revolution together with the people, were not of the people.

Lenin appeared on the scene just as this mood reached the height of its intensity. He was the leader of a minority, but it was a fighting minority organized like a detachment of storm troopers. He was an expert and ruthless propagandist who took advantage of the people's distrust, turning it against the democratic government. The February Revolution he described as a bourgeois revolution, pointing out that the reforms were slow in coming and that the constituent assembly had not yet met.

Most important, Lenin promised the people "land" and "peace." His slogan caught like fire throughout Russia, provoking mass desertions at the front, anarchy in the rear. The very word "Bolshevism," which means "Maximalism," appealed to the crowd. Actually, the "Bolshevists," or the "Maximalists" had assumed that name simply because when the Russian Communist Party split, Lenin's group drew a majority from *inside* that party. The new party thus formed called itself Maximalist. But now Maximalism acquired a new meaning: it was the epitome of extremist revolutionary aspirations, which evoked and activated what we have seen to be the Russian tendency to abandon the middle way and wander on the brink of the precipice.

When Lenin came into power he immediately put an end to the plans for the constituent assembly, the democratic, elected body which he had pretended to foster. Instead of giving the land to the people he collectivized it, and Stalin, his successor, enforced this régime by violence and terror. In fact the Bolshevist leaders, far from corresponding with the true aspirations of the Russian people, reaffirmed the old principles of absolutist autocracy. Had Pushkin been alive, he would have been able to speak once more of "scourges and chains," of the "helpless tears of slavery."

We shall not enter upon a discussion of the political aspects of Russian Communism, but in so far as we are concerned with Russian spiritual currents it is necessary to stress the ideological content of the communist myth. And first of all we must reiterate that Marxism is not a product of Russia's national genius. It is, as Pope Pius XI indicated in his encyclical on Atheist Communism, "a doctrine imposed by men often alien to the true interests of the country." It is an *imported* teaching based on Western materialism. Lenin did not seek to realize Russia's spiritual mission of love and brotherhood. He brought to Russia the system created by the German socialist Marx, who in turn had been influenced by the German philosopher Hegel and by the German atheist school of thought. In the practical sphere, Lenin had yet another teacher. As he himself admits in his writings, he applied in his revolutionary action the methods of the Prussian general von Klausewitz, the inventor of total war.

Indeed militant communism was not inspired by that desire for collective solidarity, that *sobornost* realized by the Russian

masses in the MIR and in the church. It was formulated, as the
Bolshevist theorists clearly state, according to the principle of
class hatred, with the resulting class conflict. Nowhere in Russian cultural and spiritual history do we find an ideology
informed by hatred. Petcherin hated the fetters of Nicholas's
régime, but his hatred was not directed against persons, for
his idealism was informed by the love of God.

Thus it came about that Russia was submitted to an order
profoundly uncongenial to her spiritual way of life. This became
even more obvious when the Bolshevists began to preach militant
atheism. One of the fundamental aims of the communist teaching is the destruction of religion. Lenin expressed himself very
clearly regarding this problem:

All contemporary religions and churches, all and every kind of
religious organization, Marxism has always viewed as instruments
of bourgeois reaction, serving as a defense and a doping of the
working class. . . . The struggle against religion cannot be lim-
ited to abstract ideology . . . this struggle should be brought into
connection with the concrete practice of the class movement
directed towards the elimination of the social roots of religion.
. . . The Party of the Proletariat must be the spiritual leader in
the struggle against all kinds of medievalism, including the official
religion.[1]

To the question whether this struggle might be less inevitable
if religion became "progressive," if the defects and the errors of
the historical church, the church founded *ex hominibus*, were
amended, Lenin answers, no, "there can be no good religion,
or perhaps, better religion is still more dangerous than poor
religion." These statements are quite definite and resulted in
"concrete practice"; in anti-religious propaganda and the
systematic annihilation of God conceived by Dostoievsky's
"Possessed."

No less clear are the principles of amoralism applied by

[1] *On Religion.*

Russian Communism to political and social action. We have already said that Netchaiev's *Catechism of a Revolutionary*, rejected by all previous Russian radicals, even the most extreme, was revived by the Bolshevist leaders. Thus we see Tolstoy's exalted ethical teachings and the noble ideals of the "conscience-stricken" intelligentsia succeeded by the most evil forms of Machiavellism. Transcendent moral values cease to exist. Only that is moral which serves class struggle. Such was the fundamental teaching of militant communism inspired by Lenin.

The concept of man as a free person incarnating God, as evolved by Wladimir Soloviev, disappears. Instead of a God-humanity we have a collective organism entirely submitted to the state machine. The individual is considered mere building material—a brick to be placed next to the other bricks in the communist edifice.

How did Russia react to the enforced implantation of this alien order? Today, we may state that she rejected it, though the struggle has been a long and an exhausting one and its results are not immediately apparent. The Russian people offered stubborn resistence to total collectivization of the land. This resistence caused the most terrible famines and brought about civil strife. Stalin was finally obliged to mitigate the system. He did not achieve the total collectivization he had planned; he had to grant the peasants individual plots of land which they are allowed to cultivate for their personal benefit. Though these plots of land do not exceed an acre and a half, they clearly represent a deviation from the communist farm or Kolkhoz system.

But the most resolute resistence was offered by the masses on the religious front. There have been in Soviet Russia three successive periods of anti-religious persecution. Between 1917 and 1922, that is, in the early stage of the Revolution, the Bolshevists used all the methods which they believed capable of annihilating God: churches and monasteries were closed;

the clergy was arrested and deported. Such priests as remained were deprived of the right to vote, to become members of trade unions, or to receive ration cards except those of the lowest categories. They were classified as "non-workers" and treated like pariahs. Their children were refused public education. The parishes which escaped liquidation were heavily taxed. Sacred vessels were confiscated, in spite of the energetic protest of Patriarch Tikhon, who was arrested. Priests and bishops in great numbers were imprisoned at the Solovetzk Monastery, the ancient stronghold of the Raskolniki. Members of the Catholic clergy shared the fate of the Orthodox and suffered martyrdom at their sides. The servants of Christ were executed or condemned to hard labor. Moreover, the Soviet Government sought to weaken the church by creating internal struggle, encouraging the growth of the so-called "Living Church," an anti-canonical organization nurtured by a corrupt clergy.[2]

In 1929 and 1930 there was a new wave of anti-religious persecution accompanied by a campaign of atheist propaganda. The church was grossly ridiculed in godless pageants reminiscent of Peter's "all-buffoon councils." Atheist literature, insulting posters, sacrilegious tracts and pamphlets were circulated throughout Russia.

In 1937 and 1938 Russia suffered a third period of persecution. Once more, priests were executed and deported. The Union of the Godless renewed its activity, sending propagandists and agitators to industrial plants and Kolkhozes. The members of the clergy were denounced as spies and saboteurs

[2] The Living Church, under the leadership of Archpriest Vvedensky, strove to modernize Orthodoxy through a kind of inner reformation touching upon dogma and ritual. These drastic transformations were condemned by the established Russian hierarchy. Moreover, the members of the Living Church consented to collaborate with the Communist régime, and for a time it was sponsored by the Soviet Government as a factor of rebellion against the official church. But it failed to rally the masses, and although it still has a number of adherents it is no longer encouraged by the Communists, and the majority of the Russian population, which has remained loyal to the patriarchate, holds the Living Church in suspicion. For further details see Timasheff, *Religion in Soviet Russia.*

in order to discredit them in the eyes of the people and justify the violences to which they were subjected.

All three assaults against Christianity in Soviet Russia ended in complete failure. On the eve of the second World War the head of the godless organization, Emilian Yaroslavsky, was obliged to admit that Soviet propaganda was powerless to destroy religion: all the methods had proved inefficient. Yaroslavsky's official report [3] stated that two-thirds of the peasant population and one-third of the city population remained attached to "religious superstitions."

It can truly be said that the white flame of Orthodoxy, purified by suffering and persecution, burned brighter than ever in Russia. The state church had crumbled and the magnificence of the Josephites was gone. But the spirit of St. Sergius and Nilus of Sorsk, the mysticism of St. Seraphim, survived the onslaught. The Optyna desert was closed and its monks dispersed, but the teaching of its Startzy, which lived in the people's souls, could not be suppressed.

Superficial observers who have visited the Soviet have stated that the communist doctrine has been eagerly absorbed by the masses. Uninformed newspaper men say that atheism prevails in Russia. This is a completely incorrect statement, which has been refuted by the head of the godless organization himself. Such a false picture is a result of the obscurity in which the activities of the church have been held during all these years of persecution. The Russian church has led an *underground life*. It has descended into the catacombs, putting on the "poor garb" of primitive Christianity.

Let us once more turn to Yaroslavsky's official report. The leader of the godless states that there is nothing to be gained in closing churches and expelling the clergy from their parishes, because religion is preached by roaming priests. These wanderers in Christ have for twenty-five years carried on their apos-

[3] Published in pamphlet form under the title, *On Anti-Religious Propaganda*. Moscow, State Editions, 1939.

tolate in Russia. They have founded secret communities and sung Mass in secret chapels. They have brought the sacraments to faraway, God-forsaken villages; they are eagerly expected and joyfully received by the people. Yaroslavsky writes:

The roaming priest goes about with his simple kit. It can be packed in a suitcase: censer, communion bread, a bottle of church wine, a stole—that is all that is wanted; and the servant of religion travels from village to village, wherever he is invited. If he has not been there for a year, then he baptizes all who have been born, marries all who have mated, sings Mass for all who have died.[4]

An important part in the preservation of religion has also been played by the Russian family—specifically, by the Russian woman. Children educated in Soviet public schools according to atheist principles have found in their homes the old traditions of Christian Russia. Ikons which have been carefully hidden away during the years of persecution are treasured and worshipped. And when the Testaments and prayer books were destroyed, oral tradition replaced the written word. This is why it cannot be said that Russian youth does not know God. Yaroslavsky complains in his report that Russian girls and boys still attend church services. Members of the Communist Youth Association go to Mass and even sing in the church choirs.[5]

The Soviet Government and Soviet official spokesmen have stressed, and stress particularly today, the fact that Stalin's Constitution has provided for freedom of religion. But this freedom has been restricted by the very articles of the Constitution forbidding religious teaching. Moreover, the clergy has suffered persecution in spite of the official texts. In order that the priests may be routed out without any violation of the Constitution, they have been arrested as counter-revolutionists or foreign agents.

It is a fact, however, that of recent years the Soviet Govern-

[4] *Ibid.*
[5] For further details see Timasheff, *Religion in Soviet Russia.*

ment has adopted a more lenient attitude towards religion. The priests have ceased to be pariahs; they have regained their right to vote and to send their children to schools and universities. The revival of a nationalist policy in the Soviet Union has also led to the revival of old Russian cultural and spiritual traditions. We have already seen that Alexander Nevsky, Dmitry Donskoy, and even St. Sergius himself are once more cited as national heroes, as the builders of Russia. Official Soviet textbooks openly admit that Russia's Christianization contributed to cultural growth and must be looked upon as a "factor of enlightenment."

Since Hitler invaded Russia in 1941 it may even be said that the church enjoys considerable prestige. All anti-religious propaganda has been stopped, godless publications have been suspended, and the Soviet citizens can freely attend religious services in such churches as are still open. Stalin has requested that the head of the Russian church, Metropolitan Sergius, offer public prayers for victory. The government has published a special, beautifully printed and illustrated volume describing the destruction of the churches by the Nazis. The volume contains a photograph of all the Russian prelates, wearing their traditional robes and head-dresses, a highly impressive picture. The Soviet's "new religious policy" is obviously dictated by expedience, by recognition of the fact that the church maintains the people's morale and sense of unity.

Will this new, more lenient religious policy be maintained after the war? or will the Soviet rulers return to their old party-line of militant atheism? How far is the Russian Orthodox Church cooperating with the godless rulers? Is it reviving the traditions of Dmitry Donskoy and St. Sergius, rallying and unifying the masses in the face of the invader? or is Russia returning to the régime of a state church submitted to the secular arm, as in pre-revolutionary days? All these questions arise naturally in the minds of those who are concerned with Russia's spiritual destinies. Today it seems premature to seek

an answer. Those who for twenty-five years have defended the
church in Russia against the most violent onslaughts of atheism
are better placed than we to judge of these matters.

What is obvious, however, is that the Russian clergy did not
await official recognition to carry on its mission. It has already
gained a victory, the victory of martyrdom. It has, as we have
said, achieved purification through suffering and persecution.
Today the enduring strength of Russia's soul is evidenced more
clearly than ever. For many years the destinies of the Russian
people under Communist rule were shrouded in mystery. Like
lightning flashing in the night, Hitler's blitzkrieg pierced the
gloom, and now in the flame-light of the battle we are able to
behold the people's true face.

Russian resistence has caused amazement. It has been
described as "a sacrificial ardor which has reached a breath-
bereaving scale of grandeur." [6] People with whom the reports
of journalists that communism had become the dynamic factor
of Russian society had found acceptance, have been non-
plussed, for the present heroism of the Russian people is
characterized by a spiritual intensity which a materialist doctrine could scarcely evoke. The answer to this perplexing question has been given by the great Pope Pius XI. In his encyclical
on Atheist Communism,[7] he clearly stressed the distinction
between the Russian masses and the communism which had
been imposed upon them. While condemning Russia's atheist
leaders and their doctrine, he solemnly avowed his "paternal
affection" for the Russian people.

In the light of present-day events the Pope's words appear
truly prophetic. The dynamic factor in the miracle of Russian
resistence is not communism but her thousand-year-old tradition, deeply ingrained in the Russian soul. The spirit which
created in Russia a nation able to preserve her integrity in the

[6] See Benvenisti, "Russia and Brotherhood," *Commonweal,* October
23, 1942.
[7] 1937.

face of the foreign invader who besieged the land of Alexander Nevsky and St. Sergius is drawing all her strength into unity in the face of that invader today. Once more her people have rallied for the supreme combat. Again they have heard the words which spurred them into battle six hundred years ago: "God is not in strength but in truth."

As the true face of Russia emerges from the shadows, we see once more, behind her fighting armies, the men who were her builders. It is indeed ironic that in this communist state it is the hero of long ago—Dmitry Donskoy, Peter the Great, General Suvorov, Marshal Kutuzov—who is offered as an example of Russia's greatness. Pushkin is once more the beloved poet, the oracle of the empire's might and of the genius of the people. Were Dostoievsky alive today, he would not have had to alter one word of his famous speech. Tolstoy's *War and Peace* is again Russia's "best seller" because Tolstoy left an immortal picture of Russia's national epic, the "people's war" againt Napoleon. The guerrilla fighters of today are the descendants of the guerrilla fighters of 1812.

Communism is quite out of the picture in Soviet Russia. It may still be the official régime, a new kind of state religion, to be preached chiefly by propagandists abroad, but Russia's true ideals are to be found elsewhere: in the ideology of the MIR —human solidarity, mutual responsibility in the face of emergency, the defense of the weak against the strong, brotherhood in labor and in suffering. This ideology will outlive all alien régimes. Russian resistence to Hitler is dramatic, spectacular. But the first miracle of resistence was that against Marxism. There are only three or four million men in Russia who belong to the Communist Party: there are one hundred sixty million who still bear the national tradition.

True to the inspiration of Dostoievsky's immortal novels, the masses have refused to annihilate God. They have rejected in their consciences the creed of violence and hatred. They have not accepted the happiness offered at the price of human suffering. They are not fighting for communism: they are defending their fatherland.

The Russian people have given up everything. The spirit of kenotic Christianity gives them life. It is incarnated in the starving population of Leningrad, in the men who have taken their stand in the smoking ruins of Stalingrad, in the roaming priests and in the guerrillas. All these men are "non-covetors" and "non-possessors." And they are led, not by their godless rulers, but by the Christ whom Block beheld in a prophetic vision. He is the same Christ whom another great Russian poet, Tiutchev, described in his famous lines dedicated to Russia: the Heavenly King who blesses Russia's "humble nakedness," as He walks through her poor villages in a slave's garb, crushed under the weight of the cross.

[AUTHOR's NOTE: *In September 1943, Stalin received Metropolitan Sergius and other leaders of the Orthodox Church, who informed him of their wish to call together a Council and to elect a Patriarch. Stalin stated that there would be no obstacle on the part of the Soviet Government. If a Patriarch is elected, this will mean a further and most important gain for the Church.*]

Bibliography

CHAPTER I

Fedotov, G. P., "The Religious Sources of Russian Populism," *The Russian Review*, April 1942, pp. 27–39.
———, *Sviatye Drevnei Russi*. Paris, Y.M.C.A. Press, 1931.
Golubinsky, Y. Y., *Istoria Russkoi Tzerkvi*. Moscow, Universitet-skaya Tipographia, 1901–1911.
Klyuchevsky, V. O., *Kurs Russkoi Istorii*. 5 vols. Moscow, Gosis-dat, 1923.
———, *A History of Russia*. 5 vols. Hogarth, C. J., Trans., London, J. M. Dent & Sons, 1911–1913.
Koncevicius, J. B., *The Russian Attitude Towards Union with Rome*. Washington, Catholic University of America, 1927.
Vernadsky, G. P., *Political and Diplomatic History of Russia*. Boston, Little, Brown & Co., 1936.

CHAPTER II

Borodin, S., *Dmitry Donskoy*. Kuybishev, Ogis, 1942.
Fedotov, G. P., *Sviatye Drevnei Russi*.
Khmelnitzky, S., "Alexander Nevsky i ego Vremia," *Literaturny Sovremennik*, Leningrad, 1939.
Klyuchevsky, V. O., *op. cit.*
Tolstoy, D., *Rimsky Katolitzism v Rossii*. St. Petersburg, 1876.
Zernov, N., *St. Sergius, Builder of Russia*. London, Society for the Promotion of Christian Knowledge, 1937: New York, Macmillan, 1939.

CHAPTER III

Danzas, J. N., *The Russian Church*. New York, Sheed and Ward, 1936.
Fedotov, G. P., *Sviatye Drevnei Russi*.

Karpovitch, M. M., "Nilus of Sorsk and Joseph of Volokalamsk."
    A lecture given at the meeting of the Society of the Friends of
    the Russian Orthodox Theological Academy of Paris, held at
    Union Theological Seminary, New York City, March 15,
    1943.
Klyuchevsky, V. O., *op. cit.*
Koncevicius, J. B., *op. cit.*
Kondakov, N. P., *The Russian Icon*, Vols. I–IV (with plates).
    Prague, Seminarium Kondakoviarum, 1928–1933.
Metropolitan Makarius, *Istoria Russkoi Tzerkvi*. St. Petersburg,
    Publication of the Patriarchate, 1903.
Zernov, N., *op. cit.*

CHAPTER IV

Klyuchevsky, V. O., *op. cit.*, Vol. III.
Koncevicius, J. B., *op. cit.*
Miliukov, P. N., *Otcherki po Istorii Russkoi Kultury*. Paris,
    Izdanie Sovremenye Zapisski, 1930.
———, *Outlines of Russian Culture* (Part I). Karpovitch, M.,
    Ed., and Davis, Eleanor and Ughet, Valentine, trans., Phila-
    delphia, University of Pennsylvania Press, 1942.
Mirsky, D. M., *A History of Russian Literature*. London, George
    Routledge & Sons, 1927.
Pierling, Paul, S. J., *La Russie et le Saint Siège*, "Études Diplo-
    matiques." Paris, Plon-Nourrit, 1896–1901.
Platonov, S., *Smutnoie Vremia*. Leningrad, Izdanie Vremia,
    1923: Prague, Izdanie Plamia, 1924.
Schmurlo, E. F., *Russkie Katoliki Konza XVII Vieka*. Belgrade
    Russkii Nauchni Institut, Izdanie Zapisski, 1931.
Zernov, N. *Moscow the Third Rome*, London, Society for the
    Promotion of Christian Knowledge, 1937.

CHAPTER V

Archpriest Avvakum, *Life*. Jane Harrison and Hope Mirrlees,
    trans., London, Hogarth Press, 1926.
Klyuchevsky, V. O., *op. cit.*

Miliukov, P. N., *op. cit.*

Mirsky, D., *op. cit.*

Pascal, P., *Avvakum et les Débuts du Raskol: La Crise Réligieuse au XVII siècle en Russie.* Paris, l'Institut Français de Leningrad, H. Champion, 1938.

CHAPTER VI

Bessanov, P. Y., "Jury Kryjanitch," *Pravoslavny Obozrevatel,* 1870. "Katolicheski Sviastchennik Serb (Khorvat)," *Pravoslavny Obozrevatel,* 1870.

Bielokurov, S. A., *Yury Kryjanitch po Novim Dokumentam.* Moscow, 1902.

Klyuchevsky, V. O., *op. cit.*

Pierling, P., *op. cit.*

Waldenberg, *Gossudarstvennie Idei Kryjanitcha.* St. Petersburg, 1912.

CHAPTER VII

Bielinsky, V., *Complete Works.* St. Petersburg, Biblioteka Russkich Kritikov, 1911.

Dostoievsky, F., *Complete Works.* St. Petersburg, Marx, 1894–1895: Soviet Edition, Moscow, Gossudarstvennoie Izdanie Khudojestvennoi Literaturi, 1931.

Herzen, A., *Complete Works.* 12 vols. Leningrad, Lemke, 1919–1925.

Hofman, M., "Pushkin et la Russie," *Monde Slave,* Paris, February, 1937.

Klyuchevsky, V. O., *op. cit.*

Miliukov, P. N., *op. cit.*

Mirsky, D. M., *op. cit.*

Pushkin, A., *Complete Works.* St. Petersburg, Izdanie Imperatorskoie Akademii: Nauk, 1899–1929.

Schegolev, P., *Duel i Smert Puskina.* Moscow, Gosisdat, 1928. "Sovietskye Poeti o Pushkine," *Novy Mir,* No. 1, Moscow, 1937. Unpublished material and biographical data: "Literaturnoye Nasledstvo," tomes 16–18. Moscow Academy, 1934.

CHAPTER VIII

Berdiaev, N., *C. Leontiev.* Reavy, G., trans., London, G. Bles, The Century Press, 1940.

Bogdanov, D. P., "Russkye Pissateli v Optinoi Pustyne," *Istoritchesky Vestnik,* October, 1910.

Chetverikov, S., *Optyna Pustyn.* Paris, Y.M.C.A. Press, 1926.

Danzas, J. N., *op. cit.*

Dostoievsky, F., *Complete Works, op. cit.* (letters).

———, *The Brothers Karamazov.* Garnett, Constance, trans., New York, Random House, 1933.

Gogol, N., *Bojestvennaia Liturgia.*

———, *Complete Works* (letters). St. Petersburg, Izdanie Brockhaus i Efron, 1907.

Il'in, *Sviatoi Serafim.* Paris, Y.M.C.A. Press, 1925.

Miliukov, P. N., *Outlines of Russian History, op. cit.*

CHAPTER IX

Annenkov, P., *Literaturnya Vospominania.* St. Petersburg, 1892.

Bakunin, M., *Complete Works.* 12 vols. Paris, Stock, 1907.

———, *Ispoved M. Bakunina,* Moscow, 1928.

Berdiaev, N., *The Origin of Russian Communism.* French, G. trans., G. Bles, London, 1937.

Custine, A., Marquis de, *La Russie en 1839.* Bruxelles, 1844.

Grossman, Leonid i Polonsky, V., *Spor o Bakunine i Dostoievskom.* Leningrad, Gosisdat, 1926.

Guillaume, James, "M. Bakunin," *Byloie,* No. 8.

———, *Souvenir de l'Internationale,* Vols. I–IV. Bellais et Stock.

Herzen, A., *op. cit.*

Iswolsky, Hélène, *La Vie de Michel Bakunin.* Paris, Galimard, 1930.

Mirsky, D., *op. cit.*

Nikolai, Mikhailovitch Velikyi Kniaz, *Imperator Alexander I.* St. Petersburg, Expedizia Zagotovlenia Gosudarstvennikh Bumag, 1912.

Paleologue, Maurice, *The Enigmatic Tsar.* Muir, Edwin and Willa, trans., London, Hamish Hamilton.

Panaiev, I., *Vospominania*. Leningrad, Izdanie Academia, 1927.

Panaieva, A., *Vospominania*. Leningrad, Izdanie Academia, 1927.

Pushkin, A., *op. cit.*

Schilder, N. K., *Imperator Alexander I*. St. Petersburg, Izdanie Suvorina, 1904.

Shilov, A., *Catekhisis Revoluzionera* (Nechaiev). Leningrad, Borba Klassov, 1924.

Spector, Ivar, *The Golden Age of Russian Literature*. Caldwell, The Caxton Printers, Ltd., 1943, by special permission of the copyright owners.

Steklov, J., *M. Bakunin*. Vols. I–IV. Moscow, Gosisdat, 1934–1935.

Tiutchev, F., *Poems*. St. Petersburg, A. F. Marx, 1913.

Wagner, Richard, *Ma Vie*. Paris, Plon Nourrit, 1911.

———, Collected material: *Dekabristy*. Moscow, Gossudarstvenny Literaturny Muzei Letopissi, tome 3, 1938.

CHAPTER X

Baryatinsky, Vladimir, *Le Mystère d'Alexandre Ier*. Paris, Payot, 1906.

Belyaev, *O Katolizisme*. Kazan, Imperatorsky Universitet, 1889.

Bilbassov, V., "Inozenmoie Predanie ob Alexandre Ier," *Russkaya Starina*, tome 106. St. Petersburg, 1901.

Gagarin, John, S. J., *La Russie sera-t-elle catholique?* Paris, C. Douniol, 1856.

———, *Tendances catholiques dans la Société Russe*. Paris, C. Douniol, 1860.

Gershenson, M., "Vladimir Petcherin," *Istoria Molodoi Rossii*. Moscow, 1932.

———, *Zamoguilniya Zapisski*, Mir. Kalinin, 1932.

Golovine, V. N., *Souvenirs de la Comtesse Golovine*. Paris, Plon Nourrit, 1910.

Kogan, M. S., and Hessen, S., *Dekabrist Lunin*. Leningrad, Pushkinsky Dom, 1926.

Journel, Rouet de, S. J., *Un Collège de Jésuites à Saint Petersburg*. Paris, 1922.

———, *Mme. Svetchin*, Paris.

Lemcke, Peter Henry, *Life and Work of Prince Demetrius Augustine Gallitzine*. New York, Longmans Green, 1940.

Leskov, "Iesuit Gagarin," *Istoritchesky Vestnik,* tome 25, St. Petersburg, 1886.

Lubimov, L., *Taina Imperatora Alexandra I*. Paris, Izdanie Vozrojdenie, 1938.

Lunin, M. S., *Works and Letters*. Leningrad, Pushkinsky Dom, 1923.

Maistre, Joseph de, *Complete Works*.

———, *Correspondance Diplomatique*, Paris, Levy Frères, 1860.

———, *Soirées de St.·Petersburg*. Lyons, 1836.

———, Collected material: *Josef de Mestre v Rossi*. "Literaturnoye Nasledstvo," tome 29–30, Moscow, 1937.

Moroni, Gaetano, *Dizionario di Erudizione storico-ecclesiastico da San Pietro sino ai giorni* (containing the report of Alexander's supposed negotiations with the Vatican).

Paleologue, Maurice, *op. cit.*

Pierling, P., S. J., *La Russie et le Saint Siège*.

———, "L'Empereur Alexandre Ier est-il mort catholique?", *Le Correspondant,* No. 922, Paris, February 1901, p. 796.

Polonsky, Y., "Literaturny Archiv Russkikh Iesuitov," *Vremennik,* tome 2, Paris, Obstchestvo Drusei Russkoi Knigi, 1932. "Unpublished Letters of J. Gagarin," *Vremennik,* tome 3, Paris, Obstchestvo Drusei Russkoi Knigi, 1932.

Schegolev, P., *op. cit.*

CHAPTER XI

Annenkov, P., *op. cit.*

Chaadaiev, P., *Collected Works and Letters,* Gershenson, M., Ed. Moscow, Izdanie Put, 1913. Unpublished letters in "Literaturnoye Nasledstvo," tomes 22–24, Moscow, 1935.

Custine, A., Marquis de, *op. cit.*

Gershenson, M., *Jizn i Mishlenie Chaadaieva*. St. Petersburg, 1908.

Herzen, A., *op. cit.*

Moskoff, Eugene A., *The Russian Philosopher Chaadayev*. New York, Colonial Printing and Publishing Co., 1931 (pamphlet).

Panaiev, A., *op. cit.*

Panaieva, A., *op. cit.*

Pushkin, A., *Complete Works, op. cit.*

Quenet, Charles, *Tchaadaev et les Lettres Philosophiques.* Paris, Bibliothèque de l'Institut Français de Leningrad, 1931.

Sverbeiev, D. N., "Vospominania o Chaadaieve," *Russki Arkhive,* Moscow, 1868.

Zhikharev, M., "P. Y. Chaadaiev," *Vestnik Europi,* Vols. VII–IX, St. Petersburg, 1871.

Collected material: Josef de Mestre v Rossi, "Literaturnoye Nasledstvo," tomes 29–30.

CHAPTER XII

Berdiaev, N., *Alexei Khomiakov.* Moscow, Mamontov, 1912. "The Slavophiles." A series of lectures given at the Religious-Philosophical Academy in Paris in 1933 (unpublished).

Chaadaiev, P., *Collected Works and Letters.*

Congar, M. J., *Chrétiens Désunis: Principes d'un "Oecumenisme" Catholique.* Paris, Le Cerf, 1937.

Dostoievsky, F., *Complete Works.*

———, Speech on Pushkin's Anniversary. *The Possessed.*

Khomiakov, A., *Complete Works.* Moscow, Universitetskaya Tipographia, 1900–1907.

———, *O Tzerkvi.* Berlin, Evraziiskoye Knigoisdatelstvo, 1926.

CHAPTER XIII

Berdiaev, N., *Dostoievsky.* Attwater, Donald, trans., New York, Sheed and Ward, 1934.

———, *Mirosozerzanie Dostoievskago.* Praga, Y.M.C.A. Press, 1923.

Biriukov, P., *Lev Nikolaievitch Tolstoy.* 2 vols. Moscow, Posrednik, 1913.

Dostoievskaya, A. G. (Snitkina), *Dostoievsky Portrayed by His Wife: Diary and Reminiscences of Mme. Dostoievsky.* Koteliansky, S. S., trans., London, George Routledge & Sons, 1926.

————, *Dnevnik A. G. Dostoievskoi.* Moscow, Novaya Moskva, 1923.

Dostoievsky, F., *Complete Works* (two editions cited).

————, *Letters and Reminiscences.* Koteliansky, S. S. and Murry, J. Middleton, trans., New York, Knopf, 1923.

————, *The Brothers Karamazov, op. cit.*

————, *The Idiot.* Garnett, Constance, trans. New York, Random House, 1935.

————, *The Possessed.* Cerf, Bennet A., Garnett, Constance, and Klopfer, Donald S., trans., New York, The Modern Library, 1936.

————, *Ispoved Stavrogina i Plan Jitia Velikogo Greshnika.* Moscow, Zentroarkhive, 1922.

————, *Stavrogin's Confession and the Plan of the Life of a Great Sinner.* Koteliansky, S. S., and Woolf, Virginia, trans., Richmond, The Hogarth Press, 1922.

Merejkovsky, D., *Tolstoy as Man and Artist: With an Essay on Dostoievsky.* New York, Putnam, 1902.

Murry, J. Middleton, *Fyodor Dostoievsky. A Critical Study.* New York, Dodd Mead & Co., 1916.

Spector, Ivar, *op. cit.*
trans., New Haven, Yale University Press, 1933: London, Oxford University Press, 1933.

Tolstoy, Alexandra, *The Tragedy of Tolstoy.* Verneck, Elena,

Tolstoy, S. A., *Autobiography.* Koteliansky, S. S., and Woolf, Leonard, trans., Richmond, 1922.

Tolstoy, L., *Collected Works.* Moscow, Gosisdat, 1928–1940.

————, *Complete Works.* Sytin, 1913.

————, *Krug Chtenia.* New York, Vsemirnoye Bratstvo.

————, *Lev Tolstoy i Franzia.* Collected materials in "Literaturnoye Nasledstvo," tome 31–32. Moscow, 1937. Unpublished biographical material, letters, etc. in "Literaturnoye Nasledstvo," tomes 35–38, Moscow, 1939.

CHAPTER XIV

D'Herbigny, Michel, *Vladimir Soloviev, A Russian Newman.* Buchanan, A. M., trans., London, R. & T. Washbourne, 1918.

Gerrard, Thomas, "The Russian Newman," *The Catholic World*, New York, June 1917.

Motchoulsky, C., *Wladimir Soloviev*. Paris, Y.M.C.A. Press, 1937.

Soloviev, V., *Complete Works*. 10 vols. St. Petersburg, Izdanie Obstchestvennaya Polza, 1901: St. Petersburg, Izdanie Prosvestchenie, 1913–1919.

————, *The Justification of Good*. Duddingham, N., trans., London, Constable & Co.

————, *Letters*. 5 vols. St. Petersburg, Izdanie Obstchestvennaya Polza, 1908–1911: Leningrad, Izdanie Vremia, 1923.

————, *Poems*. Published by Serguei Soloviev, Moscow, 1915.

————, *La Russie et L'Église Universelle*. Paris, Stock, Bibliothèque Cosmopolite.

————, *Russkaya Ideia*. Moscow, 1909. Collected material in "Literaturnoye Nasledstvo," tomes 37–38: Correspondence with Tolstoy. Moscow, 1939.

Stremooukhov, D., *Vladimir Soloviev et Son Oeuvre Messianique*. Société d'Editions: "Les Belles Lettres." Publication de la Faculté des Lettres de Strasbourg. Paris, 1935.

CHAPTER XV

Beketova, M., *Alexander Block*. Leningrad, Alkonost, 1922.

Biely, Andrei, *Christoss Voskresse*. Petrograd, Alkonost, 1918.

————, *Na Rubeje Dvukh Stoletii*. Zemlia i Fabrika, 1930.

————, *Natchalo Vieka*. Moscow, Gosisdat, 1933.

————, "Vosspominania o Bloke," *Epopea*, Moscow-Berlin, 1922.

Block, Alexander, *Complete Works*. Leningrad, Izdatelstvo Pissatelei, 1932–1936.

————, *The Twelve*. Deutsch, Babette and Yarmolinsky, Abraham, trans., New York, B. W. Huebsch, 1920.

Florensky, Pavel, *Stolp i Utverjdenie Istiny*. Berlin, 1929.

Gershenson, M. and Ivanov, V., *Perepisska iz Dvukh Uglov*. Leningrad, Alkonost, 1921.

————, *"Correspondance d'un Coin à l'Autre."* Du Bos, C. and Iswolsky, H., trans., *Vigile*, No. 2, 1931.

Mirsky, D., *Contemporary Russian Literature*. London, George Routledge & Sons, 1926.

Rozanov, Vassily, "Apokalipsis Nashego Vremeni." *Versty*, No. 2. Paris, 1927.

———, *Fallen Leaves*. Koteliansky, S. S. trans., London, The Mandrake Press, 1929.

———, *Legenda o Velikom Inkvisitore Dostoievskago*. Berlin, Razum, 1924.

———, *Opavshie Listia*. St. Petersburg, Suvorin, 1913–1915.

———, *Solitaria*. Koteliansky, S. S., trans. London, Wishart & Co., 1927.

———, *Temny Lik*. St. Petersburg, Veisberg i Gershuni, 1911.

———, *Uiedinenie*. Petrograd, Suvorin, 1916.

Various authors, *Vekhi*. Izdanie Zveno, 1910.

CHAPTER XVI

Basily, N., *Russia Under Soviet Rule*. London, G. Allen and Unwin, 1938.

Iswolsky, Helen, *Soviet Man Now*. London, Sheed and Ward, 1937.

Kerensky, A. F., *The Catastrophe*. New York, D. Appleton & Co., 1927.

Lenin, V., *Collected Works*. New York, International Publishers, 1927.

———, *On Religion*. New York, 1935 (pamphlet).

Miliukov, P., *Istoria Vtoroi Russkoi Revoluzii*. Sophia, Ruussko-Bolgarskoye Knigoisdatelstvo, 1921–24.

———, *Rossia na Perelome*. Paris, Imprimerie d'Art Voltaire, 1921.

Timasheff, N. S., *Religion in Soviet Russia*. New York, Sheed and Ward, 1942.

Vernadsky, G. P., *op. cit.* Collected articles and materials: "Pravda o Religii v Rossii." Moscow, Moskovskaya Patriarkhia, 1942.

Index